PRACTICING
THE PRESENCE
OF THE SPIRIT

PRACTICING
THE PRESENCE
OF THE SPIRIT

Myron S. Augsburger

Introduction by Billy Graham

HERALD PRESS
Scottdale, Pennsylvania
Kitchener, Ontario
1982

Library of Congress Cataloging in Publication Data

Augsburger, Myron S.
    Practicing the presence of the Spirit.

    1. Holy Spirit. 2. Christian life—Mennonite authors.
I. Title.
BT121.2.A79   231'.3   81-20170
ISBN 0-8361-1990-8 (pbk.)   AACR2

PRACTICING THE PRESENCE OF THE SPIRIT
Copyright © 1982 by Herald Press, Scottdale, Pa. 15683
    Published simultaneously in Canada by Herald Press,
    Kitchener, Ont. N2G 4M5
Library of Congress Catalog Card Number: 81-20170
International Standard Book Number: 0-8361-1990-8
Printed in the United States of America
Design: Alice B. Shetler

82 83 84 85 86 87 88 10 9 8 7 6 5 4 3 2 1

To the Washington Community Fellowship
with the Mennonite Church,
a visible expression
of the presence of the Spirit.

Contents

Introduction by Billy Graham — 9
Author's Preface — 11
The Nicene Creed — 13

1. Appropriating a Personal Pentecost — 17
2. Before Pentecost, and After — 29
3. Knowing the Holy Spirit as Person — 41
4. Experiencing the Presence of the Holy Spirit — 57
5. Sharing Relationship with the Spirit — 71
6. The Fullness of the Holy Spirit — 83
7. The Gifts of the Holy Spirit — 95
8. The Fruit of the Holy Spirit — 109
9. Sealed with the Holy Spirit of Christ — 121
10. Praying in the Spirit — 133
11. The Anointing of the Holy Spirit — 145
12. Witnessing in the Spirit of Christ — 157
13. The Communion of the Holy Spirit — 169
14. Confessing a Pneumatic Movement — 185

The Author — 197

Introduction

Myron Augsburger has given us a thoughtful and yet practical book on the person and work of the Holy Spirit. I am sure many will find it helpful in understanding who the Holy Spirit is and why he has been given to the church.

Alienation is one of the signs of a world which is infected with chronic spiritual sickness—alienation from God, from each other, and even from ourselves. Yet one of the central truths of the gospel is that God himself wants to dwell within us through the presence of the Holy Spirit. In this book Myron Augsburger explores the implications of this truth—a truth which should be at the heart of every Christian believer's daily experience. He rightly stresses that the Holy Spirit has not been given to believers for their own selfish enjoyment or pride, but to draw us closer to God and to equip us to do Christ's will in the world through service and evangelism.

May God use this book to challenge many Christians to deeper commitment to Christ and to help them walk in the power of the Spirit every day.

Billy Graham
Montreat, North Carolina
November 25, 1981

Author's Preface

This book is written for the whole congregation. Many books on the Holy Spirit have been written for theologians, and this is not an attempt to add to that list. Although theological insights are not lacking in this book, they are expressed in a form which intentionally emphasizes inspiration and clarity of communication.

In times of renewal in the life of the church it is imperative that biblical teaching undergirds and guides our experiences. The testing of experience is a role in which the believing community demonstrates its integrity before the Word and in covenant relationship with one another. In this role we transcend individualism to become truly a people of God.

The highest priority in Christian experience is the exaltation of Jesus Christ and his kingdom. The Spirit has come to glorify Christ in us who believe, in both worship and walk. This book attempts to hold praise and practice together, matching experience with ethics, joy with justice, and renewal with righteousness.

It is my prayer that God use this book to enrich individuals and groups in the life of Christ, remembering that the branch which bears fruit is always connected to the vine.

Myron S. Augsburger
Washington, D.C.

The Nicene Creed

We believe in one God
the Father, the Almighty,
maker of heaven and earth,
of all that is, seen and unseen.

We believe in one Lord, Jesus Christ,
the only Son of God,
eternally begotten of the Father,
God from God, light from light,
true God from true God,
begotten, not made, of one being with the Father.
Through him all things were made.
For us men and for our salvation
   he came down from heaven;
by the power of the Holy Spirit
   he became incarnate from the Virgin Mary
   and was made man.
For our sake he was crucified under Pontius Pilate;
he suffered death and was buried.
On the third day he rose again
   in accordance with the Scriptures;
he ascended into heaven
   and is seated at the right hand of the Father.
He will come again in glory
   to judge the living and the dead
and his kingdom will have no end.

We believe in the Holy Spirit, the Lord, the giver of life
who proceeds from the Father and the Son.
With the Father and the Son he is worshiped and glorified.
He has spoken through the prophets.
We believe in one holy catholic and apostolic church.
We acknowledge one baptism for the forgiveness of sins.
We look for the resurrection of the dead
and the life of the world to come.
                                   Amen.

1
APPROPRIATING A PERSONAL PENTECOST

1

Appropriating a Personal Pentecost

On one occasion, while he was eating with them, he gave them this command: "Do not leave Jerusalem, but wait for the gift my Father promised, which you have heard me speak about. For John baptized with water, but in a few days you will be baptized with the Holy Spirit."

So when they met together, they asked him, "Lord, are you at this time going to restore the kingdom to Israel?"

He said to them: "It is not for you to know the times or dates the Father has set by his own authority. But you will receive power when the Holy Spirit comes on you; and you will be my witnesses in Jerusalem, and in all Judea and Samaria, and to the ends of the earth."

After he said this, he was taken up before their very eyes, and a cloud hid him from their sight.

Acts 1:4-9.

After preaching in a community-wide crusade service one evening, I was asked the question, "Preacher, in one word what is man's greatest problem?" My answer was one word, but a long one, "self-justification!" Even in the church we tend to say, "I'm good enough as I am." And if you come to God with this attitude you will not grow spiritually until you have changed your attitude. The Holy Spirit has come to move us beyond where we are to a greater experience of

God's presence and purpose. He is God relating to us now with transforming grace.

In the words of the risen Christ just before his ascension, we have one of his final statements to his disciples. Here Jesus emphasized again the importance of the disciples' relationship with the Holy Spirit. Of all the things he could have talked about before he ascended into heaven, the one thing of importance was that in a few days they would be baptized with the Holy Spirit. But we see the human nature of the disciples. They were much like we are, preoccupied with questions of self-interest. They asked, "Lord, are you at this time going to restore the kingdom to Israel?" Jesus said, in essence, "Leave that to the Father, and to his purpose." God has a program for a kingdom far larger than national Israel. God has a plan for the future with respect to people and nations, and God is going to achieve his purpose beyond all of man's sinfulness and Satan's attempts to thwart it.

Jesus' word is for his disciples to be baptized with the Spirit! His commission is for them to go about representing God's kingdom. He said, "You will receive power when the Holy Spirit comes on you; and you will be my witnesses unto me . . . to the ends of the earth."

The passage closes with Jesus Christ's ascension to the right hand of God the Father. John Calvin says about the ascension that Jesus took humanity to heaven as the guarantee that we can be there! He also defined this as going from the physical realm to the spirit realm. But the spiritual realm is not so far away. The early church didn't think of him as so far away. There are legends that as the disciples walked the land, they would stop at the top of a hill and look off across the country as though they might see him walking to meet them.

Jesus said, "I am going away," and he did go away. Yet he

18

has come to us in the person of the Holy Spirit. The Holy Spirit made the presence of Christ real in the early church so that when they would meet together for worship, they would sit together in the spirit of prayer, saying, "Maranatha," meaning, "Lord, come." Originally it must have meant: come be with us in this meeting; come again to us. Then it began taking on the character of a prayer for the Lord's return.

Today we use the word *maranatha* as a declaration of our hope in the return of Jesus Christ. We, too, pray, waiting for that day when he will come.

Jesus also said, "I am going away, but I will send the Holy Spirit." While in his ascension he is at the right hand of God the Father, yet he has come to *us* in the person of the Holy Spirit. He is present. John writes that Jesus abides in our hearts "by the Spirit he gave us" (1 John 3:24).

We teach the children that Jesus ascended into heaven, that he is at the right hand of God the Father; then we teach them to sing, "Into my heart, into my heart, come into my heart, Lord Jesus." We may be creating a problem for them. We must explain that he comes into our hearts by his Holy Spirit. This will help them to open themselves to accept and acknowledge the presence of the Holy Spirit.

I was taught this as a boy. In my late teens, in an upper room prayer meeting at two o'clock in the morning, I came into an experience of infilling with the Holy Spirit on the campus at Eastern Mennonite College. Since then, I have seen the Holy Spirit work in the transformation of lives, in the response of people to the gospel of Christ, because the Spirit has called them. I see his work in the lives of hundreds of young people today, young people who meet as we did to pray and open their lives; and the Spirit of God fills them, transforms them, and uses them as witnesses.

19

The norm of the Spirit's work

From Acts one we note the promise of Jesus: tarry and in a few days "you will be baptized with the Holy Spirit." The answer to this promise is given in Acts 2:1-4:

> When the day of Pentecost came, they were all together in one place. Suddenly a sound like the blowing of a violent wind came from heaven and filled the whole house where they were sitting. They saw what seemed to be tongues of fire that separated and came to rest on each of them. All of them were filled with the Holy Spirit and began to speak in other tongues as the Spirit enabled them.

The remarkable thing in this happening is the fulfillment of Jesus' promise. They were baptized with and received the Holy Spirit to be present in their lives. When he came into their lives, he filled them. He bound them together in love, he transformed their lives, he created a new community. This transformation of love is *the norm* of his work. True, he wrought a miracle, fulfilling an Old Testament prophecy, a symbol, that the gospel is for all peoples. The prophet had said that in that day "with foreign lips and strange tongues God will speak to this people" (Isaiah 28:11). Paul uses this statement to explain why the Spirit gave the gift of languages (1 Corinthians 14:21). This was a symbol that the gospel is not simply for the Jewish community, but is open to people of all nations, kindreds, and languages. Further, the Apostle Paul tells us this was a mystery hid from the foundation of the world, that God intended to open his grace to everybody and not just to the Judaic community (Ephesians 3).

This new sense of brotherhood, togetherness, and community is the norm of Pentecost. When you experience the gift of the Holy Spirit in your life, you are initiated into a fellowship of "new people," of the body of Christ (1 Corinthians 12:1). In this experience of community we participate together in what it means to know Jesus as Lord. In fact, it is wrong to talk about relationship to the Spirit apart from understanding a relationship to Jesus Christ. The Holy Spirit is the Spirit of Jesus.

Further, John tells us that we are to test the spirits, to see whether what we are experiencing is of the Spirit of God (1 John 4:1). What we interpret to be a prompting from the Spirit could be another spirit—a human dimension of enthusiasm. There are psychological ways in which religion is expressed, and yet people read into them meanings of the Spirit of Christ. For example, in Acts 16, the apostle Paul had promptings to go to Bithynia, but from another spirit, not the Holy Spirit. It must have been Paul's own spirit. He also had promptings to go into Asia Minor, but the Spirit of Jesus did not allow it. Then, while he pondered this and prayed about it, he had a vision, "Come over into Macedonia." The Scripture says he discerned from the vision that the Spirit of the Lord was taking him to Macedonia. This story teaches us to always test such promptings. And to John's admonition to try the spirits, he added any spirit that does not "confess [correspond to] that Jesus had come in the flesh, is not of God" (1 John 4:1-4). This means that we can test our experience as to whether it corresponds to Jesus, to his character, lifestyle, and mission.

The necessity of the Spirit's work

One can't come to God on his own terms. Jesus said, "No one can come to me unless the Father who sent me draws him" (John 6:44). It is the Holy Spirit who convicts, the Holy Spirit who calls us. It is the grace of God expressed by the Spirit's work in one's life that moves us to God. The necessity of his work is also seen in his regenerating our lives and creating new life within us. We can't find freedom from sin by human power; it is his nature in our lives and his satisfaction that releases us from the drive to always go our own way in sin. The necessity of the Spirit's work is seen in that we can't come to God by our own power; he calls us. We can't find freedom from sin by human power; he releases us. We can't create spiritual life in our own deadness; it is the Holy Spirit who regenerates us.

It is important to be reminded of the distinct aspects of the new birth by the Spirit and of the baptism with the Spirit. The new birth, or regeneration, is the Holy Spirit taking my "dead" spirit and making it alive. That is the regeneration of my spirit. But the baptism with the Spirit is not simply renewal of my spirit but is the gift of the Holy Spirit, the Spirit of Jesus, of God, to dwell in my life. These are distinct aspects of salvation, not synonymous even though intended to be simultaneous. And although both are given in Christ, too often they are not fully understood and enjoyed by faith until some time later.

Paul M. Miller, in his book *Group Dynamics in Evangelism*, says, "The unregenerate man is a person with the top plane of his personality missing." The new birth is the creation of the spirit-dimension of fellowship with God and only the Holy Spirit creates this. We must be cautious lest we negate the Spirit's work. If we are not careful, we can resist what he would like to do in our lives. We can resist him by self-justification. We can resist him by deliberate choices when we want something that he doesn't want for our lives. We can resist him also by philosophical or theological premises which prevent his will from affecting our concepts. Often people need to adjust their philosophical bias if they are going to succeed in friendship, or in love and marriage, or in relation to the Holy Spirit.

We must also be careful lest we negate the Spirit's work by overt acts of sin. The New Testament talks about numerous sins against the Spirit. It doesn't refer only to the unpardonable sin, where some have so rejected the Spirit's work that there is no power to bring them to pardon. It also speaks about the danger of resisting the Spirit, lying to the Spirit, tempting the Spirit, quenching the Spirit, or grieving the Spirit by permitting things in one's life that dishonor the Holy Spirit.

The nature of the Spirit's work

Our convictions, if they are genuinely from God, come from the Spirit. Christianity means God has laid hold on us, not just that we hold opinions about God. Our spiritual birth has come from him. Our sanctification or the enriching of life comes from him. The nature of his work is to make us Christlike. Romans 8:29 says we are "predestined to be conformed to the likeness of his Son." It is the Holy Spirit who works to achieve that conformity in our lives, to conform us to Jesus Christ.

The Spirit works in a relational way more than in an informational manner. True, it is important to have right concepts about God and consistent expressions of theological understanding. But ultimately we are relating to Christ himself, not to concepts about Christ. To be wholly related to Christ means more than having the right ideas about him. The heart of the Christian experience is reconciliation with him, a total relationship more than simply a forensic pronouncement of being justified. We are justified in relationship, in Christ. The work of the Spirit is to attest to the relationship by his convictions, his leading, and his peace.

Witnessing to the gospel, some Christians use a relational approach, others an informational approach. The former is by its very nature more true to the gospel as it motivates persons to decisions for a relation with Christ. The latter approach is more inclined to conceptual presentations and has less evangelistic impact since it attempts to convince persons of ideas about Christ rather than put them in relation to Christ. The theology behind both approaches may be similar but the impact is quite different.

We need more than answers to questions, we need a sense of belonging. The greater issue is not whether God will now restore the kingdom of Israel; it is not whether God will help us build a great program; nor is it whether God will give us the power to be the best in a given field. We should not use God for our ends. Of course, he helps us, he enables us to be our best for him. But beware of "using God" to compete, whether in athletics, or even in building a great religious program. He helps us, not over against others but that each may be his or her best for Christ. The Spirit's work is to relate us to Christ himself as head of the church. He enables us to serve others in the spirit of Jesus. We are to seek the glory of Christ in the whole of life. As we give ourselves to God, he will conform us to the image and beauty of Jesus, a pattern which will be reflected in the social patterns of our lives.

> Blessed Master, we pray that you
> will be just that, Master in our
> lives. May your Spirit reside and
> also preside, controlling our lives
> that we might live in your will.

> Amen.

Study Questions

1. How do we understand Paul's statement that we no longer know Christ after the flesh? (2 Corinthians 5:16)

2. What is the meaning of community, of brotherhood in our experience of decision-making?

3. How can we cultivate the awareness of the Spirit's presence beyond the assurance of the new birth?

4. Is relational theology a key to maintaining a balance between the vertical and the horizontal aspects of the Christian life?

2
BEFORE PENTECOST,
AND AFTER

2

Before Pentecost, and After

> After they prayed, the place where they were meeting was shaken. And they were all filled with the Holy Spirit and spoke the word of God boldly. All the believers were one in heart and mind. No one claimed that any of his possessions was his own, but they shared everything they had. With great power the apostles continued to testify to the resurrection of the Lord Jesus, and much grace was upon them all. There were no needy persons among them. For from time to time those who owned lands or houses sold them, brought the money from the sales and put it at the apostles' feet, and it was distributed to anyone as he had need.
>
> *Acts 4:31-35.*

To know God is to walk with him in life. In fact, "no one truly knows Christ except he does walk with him in life, and no one can truly walk with him unless he knows him" (Hans Denck, *Enchiridion*, 1527). To walk with the risen Christ means to walk in the Spirit.

The intention of this chapter is to point out the remarkable change that came into the lives of the apostles when they experienced the gift of the Holy Spirit. Various passages aid our understanding of this change, the difference in a person's life when God moves in by the Holy Spirit. When

God becomes present in our lives this means that we now have the personal meaning of Pentecost. Each one must experience for himself this presence, the sovereign rule of the Holy Spirit, the one who mediates the lordship of Jesus Christ.

In relating to a person we open our life to that person in acceptance. We exchange with that person the different perspectives and ideas about life, and we are influenced by the other person. This means that one gives himself in fidelity to a relationship. In our experience with the Holy Spirit, as we give acceptance we read the Word and hear him giving us guidance from the revelation of God. We are consciously identifying and sharing so that there is benefit in our lives from the sharing.

It has been said, "A person is no more spiritual than scriptural." By this we affirm that the Scripture is the Word inspired by the Holy Spirit, that it is the Spirit's Word. As one obeys the Word, understanding it by the Spirit's illumination, he is obeying the Spirit (Acts 5:32). We do not walk in the Spirit simply by minding our feelings; we must test our emotions by the Word and its presentation of Christ. It is when we pray and seek God's leading that our lives will be "shaken" and we will be filled by the Holy Spirit (Acts 4:21). But when one is not willing to let the Holy Spirit shake up one's life, change it, or move into one's life as evidence that God is doing something fresh by his guidance, then the person will be left to the limitations of one's self.

We want to note some of the changes which came about in the lives of the disciples following their experience with the Holy Spirit. "Before Pentecost, and After" is not an uncommon notion. In the commercial world many advertisements refer to the before and after. Persons are portrayed who look one way before the product being touted is used, then there is the after shot, indicating a dramatic change. This subject offers the greatest "before and after" that we can find in history, before Pentecost and after! And what changes it makes! There are five changes to be named in this meditation on a Pentecost in one's personal experience.

Before Pentecost the disciples thought of God as "out there," but after Pentecost they knew God within.

God is no longer thought of as a person way out there, he is a God moved into our experience. Since Pentecost each can know God's presence in his or her life. God moves right into one's experience and this sense of divine presence makes a difference. We can practice the presence of God. We live with the awareness that he is here.

There are times that I have traveled far and have been on the other side of the world and Esther, my wife, has been at home, but I am never outside of the awareness that I belong to Esther and Esther belongs to me. In this sense we practice the presence of each other. In a very real sense this relational concept applies to one's experience with God. We should never be out of the awareness that we belong to Christ and he belongs to us as our Lord. And practicing his presence is a relational matter.

Practicing God's presence means that we can live with the awareness that the Holy Spirit is here. One can now pray without ceasing, one can be in conversation with God, one can practice what it means to walk with God. God is no longer out there somewhere, he has moved into one's experience. However, don't misread this affirmation; this does not mean that all there is of God is our feeling of his presence. There is a God who is *there!*—the God and Father of our Lord Jesus. And also Jesus the risen Savior is there.

31

We speak of Jesus Christ the Lord sitting at the right hand of God the Father. But he is not only someone who is *there* in that sense, but he is known *here* through the person of the Holy Spirit.

Before Pentecost the disciples were afraid of the world, but after Pentecost the world was afraid of them.

Before Pentecost the disciples were behind closed doors for fear. On the night of Jesus' betrayal in the garden all the disciples forsook him and fled. Their behavior was governed by fear. They had fear of the authorities who had taken Jesus to crucify him, fear of the crowd, fear even of the barmaid. But after Pentecost it was completely different. It says in this text, "With great power the apostles continued to witness to the resurrection of the Lord Jesus, and much grace was upon them all" (Acts 4:33). On the day of Pentecost Peter stood up with the eleven; that is, they stood up as a united body and shared the witness of Jesus Christ. We need a greater sense of boldness and aggressiveness with the gospel of Jesus Christ. I do not mean dogmatism or bigotry, but simply the bold witness, in which one, secure in his faith in Jesus Christ, is not hesitant about sharing that faith. A Quaker once said, "A man truly touched by God can influence the countryside for ten miles around."

We need the boldness to plan strategy for permeating society with the gospel of Christ. We seem to be able to plan strategy for everything else: in education, to improve programs; in business, in order to perform better each year; in our social lives, by joining associations and groups for social benefit. We do it in every dimension of life where we have concern about progress. In the Christian church there needs to be a greater sense of strategy and planning. Remember that Jesus had a strategy. In Luke 10 he sent out seventy others, two by two, before his coming. That is, he sent thirty-five teams of two members each to visit every city to which he was going to come in a little country the size of Vermont. That is strategy.

We need a better strategy for evangelism and for missions. What is your strategy to reach the people of your community? Are you winning friends among those who are nonchurch people? Has your congregation developed a strategy for home Bible studies, for getting community people in, for visitation programs? We need to become more aggressive in planning, and not be intimidated by the world.

Before Pentecost the disciples were afraid of the world, but after Pentecost something happened, the world looked on in amazement, even with a certain fear. The passage for this study follows an occasion where leaders among the apostles had been in prison, threatened and beaten, and were told not to speak again in the name of Jesus. They had answered boldly, "Judge for yourselves whether it is right in God's sight to obey you rather than God. For we cannot help speaking about what we have seen and heard" (Acts 4:19, 20).

They were bold about their declaration of Jesus Christ. They left the prison experience, went straight to the church, and called the group to prayer. And in their prayer there was no whining, no begging for God to relieve the persecution. All they asked was that with great boldness they might make known the witness of the gospel. No wonder the place was shaken where they assembled. They weren't timid people, whining because they were being persecuted or mistreated by the world. They expected that. There was an awareness that the same Spirit who guided their master was now present with them, and that this Holy Spirit would use them in the cause of witness and evangelism.

Before Pentecost the disciples were divided, but after Pentecost they were united.

Before Pentecost there had been occasions when they had argued about who was going to be the greatest. The mother of James and John had once come to Jesus to ask for a promise that, when he came in his kingdom, one son would sit on his right side and the other on his left. There was expression of this quest for greatness just prior to Jesus' crucifixion. Instead of the disciples understanding and entering into his burden with support, they were quibbling about who was going to be the greatest. When human nature takes over in one's life, it always looks out for one's selfish ambitions. But after Pentecost it was different.

Referring again to the day of Pentecost, we note that, when Peter stood up with the eleven and began to witness, they were united. Paul sums up this truth: There is "one Lord, one faith, one baptism" (Ephesians 4:5). We have enough to do in standing against the enemy of our souls to motivate us to stand together as believers. It is amazing how much energy we spend in quibbling about differences between us, energy which ought to be spent against the adversary and the powers of darkness, energy that ought to be spent promoting the kingdom. One should never become involved in exploiting or manipulating others, or in divisive things that can creep into a fellowship. We should stand unitedly with all those who confess Jesus as Lord and seek to interpret together what it means to take his lordship seriously.

Before Pentecost the disciples were defeated, but after Pentecost they knew power for victory.

Before Pentecost we get the impression that the disciples were whining about their problems. They were behind closed doors for fear. There was need in their lives for a greater sense of self-assurance and confidence. Peter was defeated, having boasted that, though all men forsake Jesus, he wouldn't. And yet he denied his Lord three times. This contrast in the lives of the disciples speaks for our experiences. How many times in our lives have we been defeated because we have not been walking in the Spirit? Opening our lives to Jesus Christ, there comes a new radiance, a new joy, a new power for victory. This was true of the disciples, for with great boldness they gave witness of the resurrection (Acts 4:33).

It is the fullness of the Spirit which enables us to live victoriously. This fullness is in proportion to our yieldedness and our appropriation of his power. In answer to the question, doesn't every believer have the Spirit, E. Stanley Jones says, "And the answer is yes. But the difference is probably this: in the new birth you have the Holy Spirit; in the fullness the Holy Spirit has you."° Before Pentecost the disciples knew about the Holy Spirit but after Pentecost the Holy Spirit indwelled them. This is the relationship which changes lives.

Instead of the defeat of living for self there was a new brotherhood, a new sharing. This was so total that it involved their very lifestyle. People who had possessions sold them and pooled the income in the church's funds so that, as people had need, they could help them as brothers and sisters. This is a philosophy which says, what is mine is the church's when my brother or sister has need. We need a cooperative economy in our fellowship, even with the forms of competitive economy. When one in our fellowship has a

---

° E. Stanley Jones, *The Way* (Nashville, Tenn.: Abingdon Press, 1946), p. 268.

lack of ability to manage well, the community of believers should recognize the Spirit's gifts of management among others and assign them to be his counselor. Stewardship does not only mean giving, it means that we are managers of God's trust.

Before Pentecost the disciples were oriented to their tradition, but after Pentecost they were oriented to mission.

This is a very basic change. Freedom comes in his mission. So often our lives have been oriented around tradition, around whatever has been passed on to us. We do things because they are traditional, or expected of us. We too easily say, "This is the way our fathers and mothers always did it." This was characteristic of the life of the Jewish community and it had become a characteristic of the life of these disciples.

But after Pentecost something superseded tradition. This doesn't mean they threw their tradition away, they were still Jewish. But what they did was to bring a greater sense of mission and purpose to bear upon that tradition. They even passed judgment upon it as to what things should change for the cause of Jesus Christ. We must hold Jesus above every tradition and get involved creatively in his mission. This includes our nationalism and our patriotism. We are now a part of his kingdom, our citizenship is in heaven (Philippians 3:30).

This call to transcend tradition must also be applied to the church at the local level. The congregation must rediscover in its fellowship a power for evangelism. People can be won to Christ by the love of a believing community. In fact, when understood as a brotherhood in the covenant of Christ—a community of love—the church itself is a part of the good news. This is an answer to our Western individualism. Evangelism is more than a one-to-one happening; it is a sharing of the dynamic of a fellowship which surrounds lonely, alienated persons with the love of the Spirit. This love gives acceptance, affirms the worth of persons, and incorporates them in a community of the redeemed who love with care.

The Holy Spirit gives newness and freshness. He has come to create new life, to create the church. We can be a part of this creative work, extending a helping hand in the Spirit of Christ.

> Father God, thank you for Jesus
> our Lord and Savior, for his gift
> of the Holy Spirit who changes our
> lives and makes us new people with
> a new mission, a new compassion, a
> new spirit. In Jesus' name.
> Amen.

Study Questions

1. What is the relation of prayer to the infilling of the Spirit? (Acts 4:31)

2. What "before and after" patterns do we discern in our fellowship as we relate to society?

3. How can we recognize the Spirit's work among us in a manner which unifies rather than implies status or rank?

4. How can the traditions which we prize become subservient to the lordship of Christ?

3
KNOWING THE HOLY SPIRIT AS PERSON

3
Knowing the Holy Spirit as Person

While Apollos was at Corinth, Paul took the road through the interior and arrived at Ephesus. There he found some disciples and asked them, "Did you receive the Holy Spirit when you believed?"

They answered, "No, we have not even heard that there is a Holy Spirit."

So Paul asked, "Then what baptism did you receive?"

"John's baptism," they replied.

Paul said, "John's baptism was a baptism of repentance. He told the people to believe in the one coming after him, that is, in Jesus." On hearing this, they were baptized into the name of the Lord Jesus. When Paul placed his hands on them, the Holy Spirit came on them, and they spoke in tongues and prophesied. There were about twelve men in all.

Acts 19:1-7.

The Holy Spirit is God, and whatever else we say about him we cannot say less than that. We are confronted with the awareness of God present in our lives. And so when we think of the Holy Spirit we think of presence and of power. We recognize this as the presence and power of the living Christ. He is continuing to do his work through the Spirit, manifesting his power, giving us the ability to do his will. But this power is not something imparted to us as much as it is the power of his presence.

41

The more dynamic changes in one's life come not through concepts but through relationships. To know God is to be in relation with him, to be identified with him by faith. His presence is the power which continues to change us.

In the 16th-century Reformation there were at least three types of Christianity, types which continue to the present. Robert Friedmann in *The Theology of Anabaptism* (Scottdale, Pa.: Herald Press, 1973) says that these three main types were sacramental, theological, and existential Christianity. Sacramental Christianity emphasized the sacraments or rites of religion as a means of grace. Theological Christianity placed primary emphasis on right doctrine, creedal statements, and God's sovereign election in grace. Existential or relational Christianity put the central focus upon one's relation with the risen Christ and his Spirit. History has demonstrated that there are values in each approach, that each should be enriched by the others.

Much of what is said in this chapter concerning knowing the Spirit emphasizes this relationship with him. Paul writes of Christ that he is the way to experience righteousness, being "the end of the law so that there might be righteousness" (Romans 10:4). As confirmation of this righteousness, this right relatedness, he pours out his Holy Spirit upon us abundantly (Titus 3:6). Through the dynamic of trust we consciously relate to him; through faith, we function in the sphere of his influence. This is a relationship with the contemporary Christ, mediated to us by his Spirit.

For the past two decades the charismatic movement has touched most denominations in the Western world. For many people this has resulted in a deep, spiritual renewal. For many it may well have introduced them to their first relational or existential experience with Christ. But for many others it has been a time of reappraisal and reaffirmation of their own earlier experience with the Holy Spirit, without an emphasis on a particular gift as evidence of receiving the Spirit. And in many third world countries the work of the Spirit has been freeing and transforming Christians without the characteristics of the charismatic movement. For many of us there is need for a clear expression of our personal experiences with the Spirit in ways other than the forms or theology of the current charismatic movement.

To say that the Christian faith is more than concepts, that it is a matter of relationship, is to say that the experience of salvation is not simply conceptual, it is relational. It is being "in Christ," living in the Spirit (Romans 8:1-14). Forgiveness is not something one gets in a package and walks away with—it is always experienced in relationship. And this very fact, the relational factor, is both a strength and a liability. It is a strength as an experience of the transforming relationship which mediates the power of grace. It is a liability when the subjective aspects of Christian experience are not balanced by a conceptual or theological understanding of experience. Every renewal in the church is accompanied by tension between experience and conceptualization of that experience. The present renewal of involvement with the Holy Spirit calls for careful interrelation of the conceptual and the experiential aspects of the knowledge of the Spirit.

In the gift of the Holy Spirit God personally moves into our lives. He is no longer a God far removed. Since the day of Pentecost, the fullness of Christ's work on our behalf is extended through the Holy Spirit as God present. The story in Acts 19 focuses on the conscious experience of the person and work of the Holy Spirit.

Here we are asked a very personal question: "Did you receive the Holy Spirit when you believed?" This question, asked by the Apostle Paul of these particular disciples at

43

Ephesus, is also asked of us. They were a religious people, yet Paul came to them with the question, "Do you know the Holy Spirit in your life?" Their answer reveals a very inadequate theology and an even more inadequate experience.

Our questions reveal much about our level of understanding. Paul's question is a valid one, not like the one by a man who, seeing a fellow dragging a chain, asked, "Why are you dragging that chain?" The fellow responded, "Did you ever try to push one?"

The people in Ephesus revealed their spiritual ignorance in that they didn't know that the Holy Spirit was being given to individuals. Paul responded, "Then what baptism did you receive?" Their answer was very honest, "We have the baptism which John preached," a baptism of repentance. Note that Paul does not affirm them as saved people needing another similar experience of grace, but rather he told them about Jesus and they believed and were baptized in the name of the Lord Jesus. Today many church members have a limited understanding of salvation, thinking primarily about the problem of guilt and need of repentance and forgiveness. Many have not entered into the new life that Jesus promises, the new life which he gives to us through the Holy Spirit. They have little awareness of the new inbreaking of the kingdom of God.

Faith identifies believers with Christ; faith in Christ engages us in relationship with him. Many people go to church Sunday after Sunday and listen to a pastor pronounce that their sins are forgiven in the name of Jesus, then go their way to live the same kind of lives, to come back again the next week to another sacramental pronouncement that their sins are forgiven in the name of Jesus. Where is the recognition of the presence of the Spirit, the presence which makes us new creatures in Christ?

We must recognize the Holy Spirit as the dynamic of God present.

The New Testament provision is for a radically different quality of life in Christ. This life is developed in us by the creative work of the Spirit. We are called by the Holy Spirit, we are converted by the Spirit, we are regenerated by the Spirit, we are indwelled by the Spirit, we are infilled with the Spirit's presence, we are to have the fruit of the Spirit, the Holy Spirit gives gifts to perform the work of Christ, and we are given the discernment and illumination of the Spirit. The central aspect is the indwelling of the Spirit which Paul expresses in other words as "Christ in you the hope of glory."

In this regard E. Stanley Jones expresses "three facts about God: (1) God for us, (2) God with us, (3) God in us. God for us, the divine Intention, the Father; God with us, the divine Invasion, the Son; God in us, the divine Indwelling, the Holy Spirit. The divine Intention becomes the divine Invasion, and the divine Invasion becomes the divine Indwelling. It is not enough to have redemptive Intention and redemptive Invasion. They are both outside of us, therefore inadequate, for our need is within us. There must be Indwelling." °

God intends that each of us experience his presence in the Spirit, the meaning of Pentecost becoming personal. This is the occasion when Jesus baptizes one with the Holy Spirit, giving the Holy Spirit to dwell in one's life. This initiates the most dynamic change that can be known in Christian experience, the reality of Christ present in one's life by his Spirit. The Holy Spirit as God in the world has come to be present in us.

° *Ibid.*, p. 274.

We should not assume that because the Holy Spirit was given to the church at Pentecost, we automatically share in the Spirit as we share in the church. We must consciously open our lives to the Holy Spirit and receive a personal Pentecost. Jesus Christ died on Calvary once for the sins of the world, but each of us comes to Jesus at Calvary and there we open our lives and experience his forgiving grace. The Holy Spirit was given by Jesus to his disciples on the day of Pentecost, but Jesus continues to baptize individuals with the Spirit as each person accepts him as Lord.

Paul's question to those disciples who had learned repentance from John the Baptist was not only valid for them, but is also valid for us. The question is, "Did you receive the Holy Spirit when you believed?" In this text the primary matter is not the time element. He is not asking of the time, he is asking about the reality. This could be read, either "*when* you believed" or "*since* you believed." Time is not the basic thing. The question is, "Do you know the Holy Spirit of God present in your life?"

The reference to baptism with water by John the Baptist is a key to understanding the baptism with the Holy Spirit. John the Baptist said, "I baptize you with water. But one more powerful than I will come, the thongs of whose sandals I am not worthy to untie. He will baptize you with the Holy Spirit and with fire" (Luke 3:16). The one doing the baptizing is Jesus. The Holy Spirit is the baptism! The New Testament speaks about the baptism *with* or *in* the Spirit, it does not speak of a baptism *of* the Spirit as though this is something the Holy Spirit does. It is Jesus who does the baptizing, Jesus is the agent, Jesus baptizes with the Spirit. What we receive from Jesus is the Holy Spirit, the Spirit is the baptism!

There is no person who can be the agent for our baptism

with the Spirit other than Jesus. Jesus Christ baptizes with the Spirit those who accept him as Lord. The meaning of the baptism with the Spirit is that we receive the Holy Spirit from Jesus to be God present in our lives, to be Jesus present in our lives by the Spirit. Following this experience we can speak of the indwelling of the Spirit, the infilling of the Spirit, the illumination of the Spirit, the anointing of the Spirit for power, the fruit of the Spirit, the manifestations of the Spirit, and the gifts of the Spirit.

The Spirit is not an "it," not a mysterious substance, not simply a divine influence. Neither is the Spirit simply a personal dimension as love, mercy, patience, and peace are personal dimensions. Rather, we speak of the Holy Spirit as person, as God present in the world as Spirit. When we relate to the Holy Spirit, we are relating to a divine personality, but not to a person simply like you and me. We are relating to Christ.

There are particular laws involved in relating to persons. We relate to persons by the laws of association, expression, and response. When we relate to the Holy Spirit, our relationship follows the same laws, beginning with association. We are to consciously open our lives to the Spirit and acknowledge him. Remember that Jesus said in Luke 11:13, "If you then, though you are evil, know how to give good gifts to your children, how much more will your Father in heaven give the Holy Spirit to those that ask him!" The New Testament also speaks of the communion of the Holy Ghost, an association or relationship of sharing.

There is the related law of expression. To know another person you must hear that person, listen to his or her expression. We get acquainted with the Holy Spirit by hearing him in the Word written, by hearing Jesus, the incarnate Son of God who brought the expression of God into the world in human form. There is no genuine way of knowing what God is like apart from Jesus. There is no genuine way of knowing what the Holy Spirit is like apart from Jesus. So the expression of the Spirit, for our communication with him, is in the Scripture as the Word written.

There is also the matter of response. This is our "yes" to God, the functional aspect of faith. The response is one of prayer, of communion, of yieldedness, of daily appropriation of his presence and power in life. Faith is response—it is an attitude which permits God to be himself in our life.

We receive the Holy Spirit as the dynamic for godly character.

There is no way that we can become godly by our own power. The new birth itself is something that happens to us. The Bible says that we must *be* born again. That is passive. We don't give birth to ourselves. We are to *be* born. This is the work of the Holy Spirit. Similarly we are to *be* filled with the Spirit; he does that, not us. We are to *be* sanctified; he does that too, not us. We do not build the kingdom, we accept it, for he is creating it, bringing its reality into our realm of experience.

It is the Spirit who works within us for godly character. He changes our lives by the new birth. He sanctifies and refines us by his work. To enhance his work we are told not to quench the Spirit, not to grieve the Spirit, not to resist him, and not to spite the Spirit of grace. Such actions are sins against the will of the Holy Spirit. On the one side we are not to negate his work, on the other side we are to open ourselves in yieldedness to him. The Spirit's work is to create wholeness in each of us, to conform us to the image of Christ. He changes us according to our best understandings of the psychology of personhood.

A Spirit-filled life is not a mystical pietistic feeling, but is the creation of whole persons, of a godliness conformed to the character of Jesus, who expressed God's will in what he was, in what he did, and in what he said. To become whole we need to know the whole Jesus, we need to know him through the disclosures of the Spirit. He has come to glorify Christ in us. Consequently our character, our values, our lifestyle, our ethics, our social relations—all are to be reflections of the love and holiness of Christ.

In this awareness we understand that the Holy Spirit has come to create a new people. This is one of the more significant aspects accompanying the baptism with the Spirit. On the day of Pentecost there burst upon the scene a new people—a new people of God living together in a new covenant, sharing the meaning of being the people of God in spirit and life. The writer of Hebrews says he has given us a kingdom that cannot be shaken (12:28)! He also adds that we are to "follow holiness, without which no man shall see the Lord" (Hebrews 12:14, KJV). Following holiness is an attitude of participation with the Holy One, with the Holy Spirit. The writer doesn't ask how holy you are, whether you have become as holy as Peter or Paul or John or Jesus. Rather, the question is, Are you *following* holiness? There is one way in which this is possible, and that is as we walk in the Spirit. Our relationship expresses our sanctification, that we belong wholly to him!

We realize that the Spirit is the dynamic for God's program.

There is no other power by which God carries on his work except that of the Holy Spirit. We speak of ourselves as witnesses or evangelists, but it is actually the Holy Spirit who is God's evangelist in the world. We are but tools in his hands. He uses us. But it is the Holy Spirit who is God's agent.

Christians speak about the church as community, a covenant community. But community is a gift of God; it is the work of the Spirit. Community is a gift of grace. We only share the genuine meaning of community when we share life in the Spirit. It is the Holy Spirit who is creating community. He relates us to one another through Christ (Ephesians 2:22).

We also need special ability to do God's work. There are gifts and abilities which only he gives. We do not develop these by our own power. They are gifts from the Holy Spirit. This dynamic power or ability to do God's work is energized through the church by the Spirit, for he does his work through people. As Paul says in Romans 12, if one's "gift is preaching, let us preach to the limit of our vision. If it is serving others let us concentrate on our service; if it is teaching let us give all that we have to our teaching; and if our gift is stimulating the faith of others let us set ourselves to it" (Romans 12:6-8, Phillips).

Such a gift-filled community is relating in covenant, participating in the new covenant of Christ. The meaning of this covenant is especially clear in Jesus' words at the Last Supper. While still in his flesh, he said, "This is my body given for you . . . this . . . is the new covenant in my blood, which is poured out for you." In these words (Luke 22:19, 20) he was saying, "I pledge myself to the death for you!" When we keep the Lord's Supper it should not be so much a sacrament as a covenant with Christ, in which we say to one another in Christ, "I pledge myself to the death for Christ and his church."

One of the functions of the community of believers is to interpret the Word together. Each fellowship of believers should be a hermeneutical community, that is, a community of interpretation. Here the authority of the Word, the Spirit, and the church come together in covenant relationship (Ephesians 1:17). The community of disciples comes to the Word with their minds already made up to obey it. They prayerfully share and seek the Spirit's confirmation as they interpret it. Here we experience his power as the Spirit of truth, as the power of grace laying hold on us, of conviction gripping us, until together we are moved by the Spirit to do the will of God. Such is the power of a group who, having met over the Word, can say, "It seemed good to the Holy Spirit and to us ..." (Acts 15:28), confident it is in the will of God.

Pentecost means power to carry on God's program, for Pentecost is person, and thus it is presence, and it is power (Ephesians 1:19-21). It is God's person, present as the Holy Spirit, releasing his power to enable us to be conformed to Christ, and to share the ministry of Christ in our society (Ephesians 3:16).

The church is called to a prophetic role in society. As members of the kingdom of Christ, we seek his righteousness above all. He calls us to love our neighbor as ourselves, to share the love of Christ with the lost, to minister to the poor in the spirit of Christ. It is this extension of the gospel into the social arena at which Christians have so often failed. The Spirit calls us to hold evangelical faith and social service together as lights to the world, as salt to the earth.

The judgment of Christ upon religious leaders of his day (Matthew 23) is relevant for us today. His woes upon the unbelieving contrast with his Beatitudes for those who hear him. Similarly Jesus said that when the Spirit comes he will convince the world of sin, and of righteousness, and of judgment (John 16:8).

He calls those of us in the West, in the midst of a society of affluence and wealth, to care for the one billion who are hungry, and the seventy million who will starve this year. He calls us in the midst of a world of violence and war, of the violation of human rights, to work for peace. He calls us in the midst of the madness of nuclear armaments adequate to destroy the world fifty times over to accept his way of peace and love. Pentecost enables us to participate in God's program; in fact, it gives us the power or authority to be his agents.

In Matthew 25 Jesus presents a scene of coming judgment for the nations. To paraphrase this in contemporary terms we could say: "I was hungry and you were obese. I was naked and you went shopping for fall styles. I was sick and you went on with your golfing. I was thirsty and you filled your swimming pool. I was in prison and you said it was where I belonged!"

The Spirit came to build the kingdom of Christ, to carry on his work. As we walk in the Spirit we will not ask God to follow our program, but we will commit ourselves to his program. We will begin each day as a commission from him, asking what he has for us to do.

> Father God, we pray that you will use
> these concepts to help persons assess
> their own experience, to look beyond
> those experiential factors which so
> often involve our attention. Quicken
> in each a greater awareness of what it
> is to be involved with the Spirit. Let
> our experience of his sovereign will
> become the controlling factor in our
> lives, in the freedom of Jesus' name.
>
> Amen.

Study Questions

1. What is the relationship between a life of continuing repentance and the new life in Christ?

2. While we fully recognize God's forgiving grace, how can we more fully enjoy his transforming grace, his enabling grace?

3. How can we move from the personal experience with the Spirit to extend this relationship to other members of the body of Christ which he is creating?

4. How can we be effective witnesses to social and political forces as his agents of peace?

4
EXPERIENCING THE
PRESENCE OF THE
HOLY SPIRIT

4
Experiencing the Presence of the Holy Spirit

> "If you love me, you will obey what I command. And I will ask the Father, and he will give you another Counselor to be with you forever—the Spirit of truth. The world cannot accept him, because it neither sees him nor knows him. But you know him, for he lives with you and will be in you. I will not leave you as orphans; I will come to you. Before long, the world will not see me anymore, but you will see me. Because I live, you also will live. On that day you will realize that I am in my Father, and you are in me, and I am in you. Whoever has my commands and obeys them, he is the one who loves me. He who loves me will be loved by my Father, and I too will love him and show myself to him."
>
> *John 14:15-21.*

The goal of history is God in the midst of his people. Creation, redemption, discipleship, and resurrection all focus on God's purpose in creating people to share fellowship with him. In fact, from the moment God created humankind everything changed for God—forever. He will always be dealing with humanity, relating to humanity. The kingdom of God is a people who enjoy his presence.

Salvation is not simply a guarantee for tomorrow, it is a relationship in the present. Jesus as my Savior saves me now from being what I would be without him. It is the Spirit in our lives who keeps effecting us for Christlikeness. Redemption is the recreation of the Imago Dei, of the truly human—God's image in human persons.

As in social life, so in spiritual life, changes in one's person are effected by his associations. From the time Esther and I were married we've never again lived by the patterns of singleness. This relationship changes the total life. So it is with the presence of the Spirit—we live in relationship with him and his presence influences us to live in the will of Christ. It is the presence of God in one's life which is the power to transform us and make us different people. We can't stay where we are if we are children of God, walking in the Spirit. He always calls us beyond ourselves to new realities and new dimensions of grace.

Jesus, in the high priestly prayer of John 17, said, "Thy word is truth." There is no other source of correct knowledge of God or his will; the truth of God is in Jesus as we meet him in his inspired Word. And there is no way to know how to discern the work of the Holy Spirit apart from the Word of the Spirit. The same Holy Spirit who inspired the Book works in our lives through the Book. This is what makes the Bible so unique; the author is alive and he is present. The approach of faith is to come to the Bible with one's mind already prepared to obey it. The task is to understand and to apply it. And as we come with openness to the Spirit's illumination, we can discern what God is asking and, by his grace, live accordingly (Ephesians 2:10).

Some of the most sublime and clearest teachings on the person of the Holy Spirit are in the Gospel of John. In chapter 14, we have two remarkable affirmations by Jesus about the Holy Spirit and his work. The one is the promise of another comforter or counselor, one who comes to stand with us and in us. He understands, he can mediate the meaning of God's grace in our lives, and interpret that grace to us (John 14:16-18).

The other affirmation is similar and comes from Jesus' promise as he looked forward to his resurrection. He says of the coming of the comforter, "On that day you will realize that I am in my Father, and you are in me, and I am in you" (John 14:20). This sounds somewhat mystical, yet it is a relational statement. Jesus is in the Father in being fully identified with him. And we are in Jesus by being completely identified with him. Then he says, "I in you," meaning that he, by the presence of the Holy Spirit, will fully identify with us. This is the wonderful thing about Pentecost, about the baptism with the Spirit. By faith we know his indwelling presence, and we experience the fullness of the Spirit in our lives.

The Spirit of God changes people's lives by the power of presence.

When we have problems such as carnality, complacency, or a character that is less than Christlike, the Holy Spirit works to correct these problems.

He corrects *our carnality* by his convictions, calling us to a higher level of spiritual experience, to follow holiness as an answer to our selfishness. Carnality, the pattern of persons going their own way rather than God's way, will end with total surrender to Christ.

At the Lausanne Congress on Evangelism, I heard Malcolm Muggeridge speak of his own experience of new life in Christ. "Confined in the tiny dungeon of my own ego, shackled by the inordinate demands of the will, the window of my soul let in the light of Christ, of reality, of love, of freedom; but I must keep looking into that Light!" And that light for freedom and love is in the work of the Spirit through whose presence "the love of God is shed abroad in our hearts" (Romans 5:5).

As E. Stanley Jones has said, "What happened in history must move straight on inside of us in experience of the Indwelling, must do it or fail. The historical must become the experimental. Otherwise the Christian faith is a counsel of perfection, making impossible demands on human nature. But if the divine Indwelling is a fact, then everything is possible.... God apart from us can do little. We apart from God can do little. Together we can do anything."°

The Holy Spirit deals with the problem of *our complacency* by his creative work. One can't truly know the life of the Spirit and still be complacent. The Holy Spirit leads us to become actively involved in his work of building the kingdom, calling people to Christ. One who is Spirit-filled doesn't simply live to make a living. One who is Spirit-filled makes a living so he can get about the Father's business. The Apostle Paul, speaking about this in Ephesians, says that in contrast to stealing we work, so that we have to give (4:28). Walking in the Spirit means that instead of complacency one gives himself to vital involvement in the Holy Spirit's work, calling people to Christ. Our mission is to bring Christ to the world, to create a new people of God in the world, to be witnesses in society.

But beyond dealing with problems of carnality and complacency, he works for the development of *character*. While we may make resolutions, or work to improve our character and our dispositions, our success is limited. We have problems of impatience and we express anger about things that don't merit that much emotional feeling. We are tempted to compromise our beliefs or exaggerate for impression. We

---

° *Ibid.*, p. 268.

have problems such as envy, jealousy, and lust. How does one find correction for these? There are habits that one may acquire in life that are often easier to drop than to make changes in one's character.

Some psychologists say that a person's personality is plastic until he is thirty-five. After that, unless one has cultivated openness to change, it is very difficult to change. You may know the reference to a sign on the old road to Alaska which read, "Choose your rut well, you will be in it for the next twenty-five miles!" Many people have been in the same rut for a long time.

The answer as to how we make changes in our lives is that the Spirit of God can enable the change. At times we meet people who have been cantankerous individuals, but something has happened and they now are loving, companionable, gracious persons. All we can say is that they have been touched by God.

The Spirit of God answers the spirit-problems at the deeper level in our lives.

Jesus said that when he comes, "he will bring glory to me by taking from what is mine and making it known to you" (16:14). This is far more than merely being religious. In fact, our master never used the word "religion." The Holy Spirit did not come to make us "religious," but he has come to glorify Christ in and through our lives. He has not come to glorify us, or our abilities, or our religious experience, but to glorify Christ.

If we should use our experiences with the Spirit as spiritual status symbols or have certain gifts or manifestations that we flaunt as the symbols of how spiritual we are, the Holy Spirit will pull the rug out from under us. We must, in humility, turn again to the lordship of Jesus Christ.

61

The Holy Spirit will work where Jesus is glorified. Where Jesus is not glorified, he will not do his work. It is said, "God is unlimited as to what he can do through a person who doesn't care who gets the credit." The Holy Spirit has come to do one thing, to glorify Christ.

When we talk about experience, we are talking about a variable, because we are such different personalities. We each bring to a given experience the whole background of what has happened to us and in us, coupled with our choices and aspirations. This creates a new kind of synthesis of mental, emotional, and social expression. That is what we call experience.

If I tell you that I speak out of the experience of marriage, all you know is that I am a husband, a lover, and a father. And that is true. But you do not know how Esther and I express our affection to each other. You don't know whether it is a "drapery" affection, or a more dignified, or even formal, expression of affection. You don't know the variables of our experience. All that you can know by the word experience is that I am involved. When I say that I have had an experience with the Holy Spirit, that Jesus gave the Holy Spirit to me to live in my life, you don't know the personal implications of that experience. All you know is that I experience the Holy Spirit's presence and fellowship, his communion and fruit, his gifts at work in my life. You know only that I am involved with the Holy Spirit in and through Jesus Christ.

The Apostle Paul writes of the importance of our "being renewed in the spirit of our minds." He says that we are to "be transformed by the renewing of your mind" (Romans 12:2). This is a work of the Holy Spirit, enabling us to perceive the truth of God through his Word written. This is beautifully affirmed in 1 Corinthians 2:12, 13:

> We have not received the spirit of the world but the Spirit who is from God, that we may understand what God has freely given us. This is what we speak, not in words taught us by human wisdom but in words taught by the Spirit, expressing spiritual truths in spiritual words.

It is this work of the Spirit in our intellects which leads to "faith seeking understanding." He opens the mind to understand the truth of grace, the covenant of love, the essential nature of the Christ. In so doing he opens for us a new understanding of ourselves and of where we are in relation to the economy of grace.

The spirit of one's life has to do with the deeper aspects of personhood. We are not what we think we are, we are what we think! And when our reflection or meditation is understood as essential for the development of our personalities, we can by wholesome thinking enrich the inner self. As Solomon said, "As a man thinketh in his heart, so is he" (Proverbs 23:7, KJV). Paul writes that we are to "be renewed by the Spirit in the inner man." The Holy Spirit interacts with our spirit for wholeness, peace, and joy. Just as the presence of a good friend enriches one's mood, so the awareness of the Spirit's presence affects one's spirit.

Going deeply into Christ means opening one's insecurities to him. It is daring to be honest and candid about one's self. It is refusing to live in a fantasy world. It is taking off the masks, including the one we wear for our self-image. The spirit of one's life is sanctified when we open our inner hidden self to God, and let him be master of all. Only in this way will we become engaged in personality inventory with the Master's analysis. Easy answers at the hands of manipulatory persons who play with your emotions will never reach this deeper level of security in Christ nor conformity to him.

Mood and disposition are aspects of one's person which

are not easy to control. In fact, they are quite dependent upon fellowship and a feeling of worth. If we feel rejected or engage feelings of failure, our mood becomes "dark" and our disposition negative. But being loved and loving has the power to transform one from despair to joy. It is the fellowship of Christ, in the Spirit, which lifts us by spirit answering to Spirit. A unique expression of this truth is in Paul's prayer in Ephesians:

> For this reason I kneel before the Father, from whom his whole family in heaven and on earth derives its name. I pray that out of his glorious riches he may strengthen you with power through his Spirit in your inner being, so that Christ may dwell in your hearts through faith. And I pray that you, being rooted and established in love, may have power, together with all the saints, to grasp how wide and long and high and deep is the love of Christ, and to know this love that surpasses knowledge—that you may be filled to the measure of all the fullness of God.
>
> Now to him who is able to do immeasurably more than all we ask or imagine, according to his power that is at work within us, to him be glory in the church and in Christ Jesus throughout all generations, for ever and ever! Amen.
>
> *Ephesians 3:14-21.*

The Spirit of God accommodates himself to the cultural and emotional aspects of our experience.

Experience, being subjective, is a variable in people's lives, dependent upon our conditioning. In the years of my ministry, counseling with people, I have found that people relate to people on different levels. There are some persons who relate to other persons almost completely at a sensory level. For example, some people run their courtship like a petting party. It is unfortunate when a marriage is built only on sexual attraction between persons, and then later, when they find that they need much more for communion, fellowship, and interchange, they have nothing in common between them except the sex experience. That experience is well and good, for God intends that it be good, sanctified by his blessing and enjoyed in love. But there is more than that between a man and woman. They ought to be the best of friends and they ought to be free in communicating and sharing.

Others relate to people at an emotional level. If I may use the term "psycho-emotional," it will suggest the larger dimensions of the emotional level, including the psychological and intellectual aspects of one's life. At this psycho-emotional level there is a more holistic involvement of the personality. Many persons relate to others primarily on this level.

Third, there are persons who relate to other persons at a more spirit level, with awareness of belonging, acceptance, and communion. This level has to do with consciousness, with vision, with purpose, and with the deeper sense of participation and fellowship.

When God wants to get through to an individual, he will doubtless come through at the level authentic for a given person. If the individual knows how to relate to other persons only at a sensory level, God, who cares so much about persons that he is more concerned about getting through to the individual than he is about the particular form of the experiential dimension of that relationship, will logically come through at the sensory level. But when God comes through to someone who relates at a more spirit level of awareness and consciousness, God will meet him at that level. This, I believe, accounts in part for different types of spiritual experiences.

We should note, however, that Paul wrote to the Thessalonians, praying that they might be sanctified by the Spirit through and through, spirit, soul, and body (1 Thessalonians

5:23). We need a holistic experience, for we are unified beings. This would mean that the Holy Spirit, at whatever level we come into experience with him, will seek to permeate our total lives with his presence.

One of the central aspects of Christian experience is praise, or worship. A person is what he or she worships. Consciously or unconsciously, our lives are fashioned by our worship priorities. Praise is a key to sanctifying the spirit of one's life. Praise lifts one's inner being to adoration of God. In doing so one has his priorities focused. It is in worship, in the exercise of reverence, that one is put in tune with the highest reality. We read in Hebrews 4:12, "The Word of God is living and active. Sharper than any double-edged sword, it penetrates even to dividing soul and spirit, joints and marrow; it judges the thoughts and attitudes of the heart." As we worship, in the Word and Spirit, he will divide between that which is merely "soulish" (personal ambition) and that which is of the Spirit (divine affirmation). Obedience is not primarily walking by a code but walking in the Spirit in praise.

It is important to focus attention on how the term "baptism *with* the Spirit" has been interpreted in this discussion. I have not spoken about a baptism *of* the Spirit as though the baptism is. something which the Spirit does. We can properly speak of an anointing of the Spirit, an infilling of the Spirit, fruits of the Spirit and gifts of the Spirit; but it is a baptism *with* the Spirit. The Spirit is the baptism, Jesus does the baptizing. The power is the Spirit's presence.

In the Christian church there are at least five ways in which the baptism with the Spirit is interpreted. First is the *historical interpretation*, that the baptism with the Spirit happened once on the day of Pentecost and the Spirit has been in the church ever since and we share in the Spirit as we share in the church. A second is the *Wesleyan interpreta-*

tion, that the baptism with the Spirit is for sanctification and is experienced as a "second blessing" beyond justification in which the experience of the Spirit releases us from all inner tendency toward sinning. The third may be described as the *R. A. Torrey approach:* the baptism with the Spirit is a special endowment with power for witness and soul-winning. (Some Pentecostal groups interpret this as the third work of grace, or "third blessing," with tongues.) The fourth is the *charismatic emphasis,* or a baptism "of" the Spirit as a distinct happening in which the Spirit gives particular manifestations or is evidenced by particular gifts. The fifth is the *relational emphasis,* interpreting the baptism with the Spirit as the occasion when Jesus, the one baptizing, gives the Holy Spirit to those who accept him as Lord. He thereby becomes master in their lives.

Too often we maximize our interpretation of the experience in which one receives the Spirit, and we minimize the life in the Spirit, or the fellowship of the Spirit. Analyzing one another's experiences does not appear to be one of the gifts of the Spirit! True, there is the gift of discernment of spirits, to know whether a happening is of God or not. However, we respect the sovereign right of the Spirit to come to people in ways that are authentic in their realm of experience. It is for us to respect this variety, knowing that he manifests his work "according to his will" (Hebrews 2:4). To know him is to know Christ, to know God himself, to bow before his sovereign will. Let us seek to know him and to have joy in his fellowship.

> Help us to seek you in longing,
> And long for you in seeking;
> To find you in loving, and
> To love you in finding.
> —*St. Anselm*

Study Questions

1. How does our openness to the Holy Spirit help us to be more open with each other? How can our sharing openly with one another teach us more about being open to the Spirit?

2. How can we relate the Spirit's presence to our ethical decisions in the practice of love toward others?

3. How can we find the release from self-centeredness to joy in times of moodiness or depression?

4. How can we assess the various levels of our experience with the Spirit and enjoy this reality without judging the experience of others?

5. In discussing the various ways in which the baptism with the Spirit has been taught, how can we affirm the reality of each of us relating personally to the Spirit while expressing this meaning in different ways?

5

SHARING RELATIONSHIP WITH THE SPIRIT

5

Sharing Relationship with the Spirit

But I tell you the truth: It is for your good that I am going away. Unless I go away, the Counselor will not come to you; but if I go, I will send him to you. When he comes, he will convict the world of guilt in regard to sin and righteousness and judgment: in regard to sin, because men do not believe in me; in regard to righteousness, because I am going to the Father, where you can see me no longer; and in regard to judgment, because the prince of this world now stands condemned.

"I have much more to say to you, more than you can now bear. But when he, the Spirit of truth, comes, he will guide you into all truth. He will not speak on his own; he will speak only what he hears, and he will tell you what is yet to come. He will bring glory to me by taking from what is mine and making it known to you. *John 16:7-14.*

The true Christian disciple is a Spirit-indwelled person. One is not a Christian simply by imitating Jesus, but by being reconciled to God through him. Jesus wasn't only an example, he is Redeemer and Lord. He is the one who reconciles us to the Father. We don't have the power to become another little Jesus. There is something wrong with us. We are sinful. We need a Savior. And we need the Savior to save us from being today what we would be without him today.

At Eastern Mennonite College, where I served in administration, the goal is to educate informed disciples. We mean by this *disciples* of Jesus Christ, persons who identify with him and learn from him as master. We also mean *informed*, for we believe that living in our kind of world Christians cannot be intellectually careless or shoddy. We need to understand the times to be able to communicate the gospel, and we need the best understandings possible, so that our character and personality can be as full of the expression of the grace of God as He enables us to achieve. But the agent in all of this is the person of the Holy Spirit, in whom we are relating to God as he is known in Christ.

Discipleship is learning from and identifying with the Master. It is the relational aspect of faith. To be a disciple is to follow Christ daily in life. That which keeps this from being a mere imitation of Jesus is the awareness of the Holy Spirit being present with us now.

This is discipleship in grace, for we do not have the ability to be Christlike. But in grace the Spirit is present to mediate to us the ability to do his will! He convicts, prompts, and guides us in the will of Christ.

Discipleship is not static, it is dynamic, a daily following in decisions which glorify Christ. Being fully aware of his lordship means being a participant in his kingdom. Consequently, we live as pilgrims in this world, putting his kingdom above every other purpose and loyalty. The Spirit has come to continue God's work in the world through us!

The Bible refers to our teacher as the Spirit of truth. We can only discern unveiled truth, the evangelical truth of the gospel, by the Spirit's illumination of the Bible. There is a truth anyone can seek in a laboratory or classroom, that is discursive truth, truth about things. But the truth of God is known only in his own self-disclosure.

72

When we want to know the full truth about a person, we must meet the person; and the person must open up and reveal or disclose himself. Short of this we don't understand the real person, to know what makes him or her tick. So it is with our knowledge of God. You never understand God just by philosophical speculations about him. You only understand God by coming to him and letting God reveal himself to you. God has done this in Jesus Christ. Now the Holy Spirit takes the truth *about* God and makes this the truth *of* God in our experience.

Knowledge *of* a person is different from knowing something *about* a person. Knowledge *about* a person is only a limited knowledge, but to have knowledge *of* a person is an intimate, deeper kind of knowledge.

The passage in John 16 is a promise of the coming of the Holy Spirit and a disclosure of how he will work. Jesus said that he needed to go away so that the Spirit could come. While Jesus was here as the Son of God, God was localized in Jesus of Nazareth. But in the risen Christ, the ascended Jesus sent the Holy Spirit, who is not localized in one human form. He is involved in the total world, transforming the lives of people around the globe. Further, it was important that Jesus go away so that we would do "transfer thinking," begin thinking of what it means to live and walk in the Spirit rather than simply copy his patterns. We are "spirit beings" in these bodies, and we can have a spirit relationship.

Jesus said that when the Spirit is come, he will convince the world *of sin* because they did not believe in him (John 16:8, 9). The implication is that we believe on him, and by our witness the Holy Spirit convinces the world of their sin of not believing in Jesus. Next, Jesus said the Spirit will convince the world of *righteousness*, because "I go to the Father, and they see me no more." The implication is, they will see his disciples. By our righteous living or walk in the Spirit, the world becomes aware that righteousness is a possibility in the grace of God. Further, he said the Holy Spirit will convince the world of *judgment*. Notice, He did not say, of judgment to come. He said of judgment now, "because the prince of this world is judged." As we live in victory rather than submit to the influence of Satan, we demonstrate to the world that Satan is already judged and defeated, and men don't have to live under his control.

In a non-monotheistic culture this is especially relevant, for they do not have the concept of sin common among theists. They think rather of the negative realm being that of demons. Similarly Paul said, we are translated from the kingdom of darkness into the kingdom of his Son. Paul wrote in Ephesians 2:1, 2:

> As for you, you were dead in your transgressions and sins, in which you used to live when you followed the ways of this world and of the ruler of the kingdom of the air, the spirit who is now at work in those who are disobedient.

Paul affirms a transformation, a release from the power of darkness into the liberty of the Spirit of God.

Jesus said that when the Spirit of truth is come, he will guide his disciples into many things that they were not ready to receive at that point. Now we can enjoy the things which the Holy Spirit led the disciples to understand. The book of Acts and the epistles explain how the Holy Spirit interpreted Jesus to the disciples. Jesus was limited as to what he could communicate in the Gospels because of that particular stage of God's disclosure. The world had not yet experienced the crucifixion and resurrection of Jesus. Also, there was a limitation on the part of the disciples to understand the full meaning of God's grace. But following the resurrection Jesus could send the Holy Spirit, and we now take seriously the presence and work of the Spirit in our personal relationship with Christ.

The Holy Spirit is a person to be accepted.

Today there is a prominent emphasis on the word "acceptance." If the Spirit is a person, then we know him by giving acceptance to him. Someone may say, "Didn't I receive all of this in the new birth? Is there something more that I am to receive?" The answer can be best seen in relationship to a person. In marriage we have a classic illustration. When we marry and share a honeymoon, knowledge of each other is very limited compared to what it is five years later. Our knowledge of one another is exciting and growing as we discern more about each other. This is because we keep giving acceptance to one another, opening up new facets of our lives and our sharing. In a similar way, while we come to Jesus and accept him as Lord, all that he has is ours, but we can't experience it all at once. We don't have that capacity. Nor is that possible in the psychology of personality development, nor of nurture in education, nor of relationships such as in this illustration of marriage. We can't absorb everything in a moment from another person.

Relating to the Holy Spirit means that we have begun that relationship in the experience where Jesus baptizes with the Spirit, or gives the Spirit to dwell in our lives. But we must recognize that the Holy Spirit is a person to whom we give acceptance. And we don't do this only once. We keep giving acceptance.

Those who are married understand this. Persons in friendship know this. But if there are times when there is a little tiff or difference between two people, and they turn on the silent treatment and close each other out, that impairs the

75

relationship. The only way this is remedied, and we return to the harmony intended in our sharing, is when we begin giving acceptance to one another again. In the psychology of counseling we stress the importance of giving acceptance to other people and to people with whom we differ. So also in the spiritual life: the Holy Spirit is a person to be accepted, and this means having an attitude of giving acceptance.

I remember a story of D. L. Moody being invited to a city for an evangelistic crusade. One of the ministers of the committee who wasn't so excited about such a meeting asked, "Why do we have to invite D. L. Moody here? Does he have a monopoly on the Holy Spirit?" One of the other ministers replied, "No, D. L. Moody doesn't have a monopoly on the Holy Spirit; the Holy Spirit has a monopoly on D. L. Moody." And that is the key. If you give acceptance to him, he can fill your life, he can become the Spirit in control.

The Holy Spirit is a presence to be acknowledged.

When he is present in our lives, we don't ignore him. We don't take him for granted, failing to consciously relate to him. This can be illustrated again by marriages where people come and go, taking one another for granted, not expressing love, acceptance, and the feeling they ought to have for one another. Each one's role becomes routine and there is no excitement, no interchange, and no creativity. Similarly people appear to have this problem in their spiritual experience, for having come to Jesus for salvation, they don't know much about the Holy Spirit's work in their lives. We must not presume on the Holy Spirit, he is a presence to be acknowledged, to be recognized and enjoyed.

For any meaningful interchange between several personalities there must be conscious regular association. To take one for granted is a sure way to have a friendship or marriage atrophy. Similarly, persons in whose lives there is joyous evidence of fellowship in the Spirit are persons who concentrate less on the "unusual happenings" of that relationship and who concentrate on the fellowship itself. Paul says, "If we live in the Spirit let us walk in the Spirit" (Galatians 5:25).

My friend, the late Dr. Walter Wilson, illustrated this in the following way: suppose that I should call the conservatory of music for a teacher in piano. The teacher comes out to the house and says, "I've come to give you piano lessons." And so we sit down and begin and suddenly I have a question. I jump up and run to the telephone and call the conservatory and ask them for an answer to my question. They would say, "Didn't we send a teacher out to you?" "Yes." "Is the teacher still there?" "Yes." "Then why don't you ask the teacher?" In our experiences people ask God over and over again for guidance when the Holy Spirit is right here, and what we need to do is open our lives to his guidance, test our promptings by the Scriptures, and live by the principles of his Word.

The Holy Spirit is a power to be appropriated.

There is power in love, power in joy, power in fellowship. To enjoy his power at work in our lives we must take it by faith. If you have a problem of lust, ask the Holy Spirit to be your purity. If you have a problem of discipline, begin with his inner disciplines. Appropriate his power. His power can overcome our selfishness.

You can illustrate this by holding a book out, feeling the pull of gravity on the book, knowing it would drop if you didn't hold it. But you are so much stronger than the pull of gravity on that book; and it can't fall, you have it. In a similar way Paul writes to the Galatians in chapter 5, verse

17: The self is always there like the pull of gravity, desiring to go one way, but the Holy Spirit is always there like your hand lifting the book, saying, no, we're going this way, so that you can't do what you would have done if the Spirit wasn't present! The Holy Spirit is present and his power leads us in his direction. The Holy Spirit is a power to be appropriated.

The key to this power is obedience. There is no shortcut, nor lesser way to his power. As Bonhoeffer says, "Only he who believes is obedient, and only he who is obedient believes." His power is for those who obey him. It is obedience that liberates one from one's self, that frees one to relate to larger spheres than his own opinions and greater power than his own ego. One is only liberated to love when one obeys the principles that place supreme value on others and is thus released from the limiting grip of selfishness.

Similarly we can be liberated from being controlled by a problem. We may still have the problem, but whatever our problem he will work with us in the problem, transforming our approach to it, and release us from being dominated by the problem. Then he gives us a new freedom to cope with it. The Holy Spirit is God's power at work in one's life, the ability to do God's will. This doesn't mean he sweeps the problem away, but he gives us the ability to do God's will in it. He can replace the problem with the fruit of righteousness until God is glorified in us.

> Father God, thank you for the gift of the Holy Spirit. Blessed Master, thank you for giving us the Spirit to be present in our lives. Blessed Spirit of God we acknowledge you today and pray you will fill us with your power and wisdom. In Jesus' name.   Amen.

Study Questions

1. How does discipleship differ from pietism or mysticism in faith?

2. Can one be active and aggressive about the will and work of God without falling into legalism or "works righteousness"?

3. In what ways is the Spirit working through the church to "reprove the world of sin, and of righteousness, and of judgment"?

4. How can we relate the power of the Spirit and our psychological awarenesses of our strengths and weaknesses so that we experience the victory of grace at the varied levels of our life experiences?

6
THE FULLNESS OF THE HOLY SPIRIT

6

The Fullness of the Holy Spirit

> Do not get drunk on wine, which leads to debauchery.
> Instead, be filled with the Spirit. Speak to one another with
> psalms, hymns and spiritual songs. Sing and make music in
> your heart to the Lord always giving thanks to God the Father
> for everything, in the name of our Lord Jesus Christ.
>
> *Ephesians 5:18-20.*

We humans try to be so very self-sufficient. We go our
own way, acting as though we don't need God or religion.
But we are really not self-sufficient. Take a look at our society, we're self-sufficient except for alcohol—we have a
million alcoholics. We're self-sufficient except for how to live
with our drives in the area of sexuality—we have fifty thousand unwed mothers and 44 divorces for every 100 marriages, and all types of promiscuity, including both pre- and
extra-marital sex relations. We're self-sufficient except for
despair—we have 25,000 suicides a year among young
people alone. We're self-sufficient except for our passions
and hatred, for in our society we have hundreds of murders,
and we don't know what to do with the problem of crime.
What is it that humans need to change in their lives?

There is no power in the world as enriching as that of the

Spirit of Christ. And there is no word in the world so great as the gospel, the Word or sword of the Spirit. And there is no experience in the world so great or so wonderful as to open one's life to Jesus Christ as Lord and let the Holy Spirit transform one's life. But beware of trying to "use" God. Beware of thinking of salvation as an insurance policy, as a guarantee that you will make it to heaven and miss hell, as though God can stand back while you run your own life. Beware of trying to manipulate God. And beware of thinking that you can manipulate the Holy Spirit as though experiences with him are to be a private pietistic experience with great enthusiasm or ecstatic expressions. Beware of using the Holy Spirit as though you need his particular expressions, gifts, and power for your own spiritual status. We must beware of using our experience as a status symbol.

When we speak of knowing the Holy Spirit in our lives, we are speaking about God being here. And this is not always a comfortable experience. God can be very discomforting. His presence orders one's life more thoroughly than any system of laws. The presence of the Holy Spirit is the most searching thing that one can experience. He comes as God present, as God resident in one's life. This means that we give up controlling life by our own power and open ourselves to his power. We confess that we are not self-sufficient.

And so our theme—"The Fullness of the Holy Spirit." People at times ask the question, "Are you filled with the Spirit?" In fact, that question can be one of the most pointed questions faced by any Christian, but it is also a very difficult one. For one to affirm that he is filled with the Spirit is a very difficult personal judgment. I would rather that some other person said, "He is a Spirit-filled man," than for me to say that I am filled with the Spirit. This could simply be a boast, rather than an honest expression. The one who knows the fullness of the Holy Spirit in his life, at the same time also knows that the greatness of this experience calls for more sharing with the Spirit. Such persons are the last to affirm that they have really experienced all of the fullness that they want in their lives. In fact, A. W. Tozer said, "One who thinks himself to be the chief of saints, may in reality be the chief of sinners. And one who thinks himself to be the chief of sinners (like Paul), may in reality be the chief of saints."

In the brief passage at the outset of this chapter, Paul speaks of the Spirit, of Jesus Christ as Lord, and of God the Father. This is an expression of God as Father, as Son, and as Spirit. When we think of the Trinity, we should not think of the Trinity mathematically. When we talk about the oneness of God, we do not mean a numerical one. There is a greater oneness in the three expressions in which there is the unity of God, than if we had to talk about oneness simply as a mathematical one. In a similar way, when we talk about the Trinity we should not think of Trinity mathematically, as though we were talking about a mathematical three. The three-ness has no such separation within it that counteracts the oneness. We affirm that God is known as Creator, Redeemer, and Sanctifier; as Father, Son, and Spirit. The oneness of God is expressed in the way these three manifestations unite to be that one God, to whom we give our allegience and loyalty.

God is known supremely in his revelation in Jesus Christ. We experience him as he mediates himself to us by the Holy Spirit. Paul writes, "Be not drunk with wine, in which are all kind of excesses, but be filled with the Spirit" (Ephesians 5:18). In the Greek this verse is in the present tense and the imperative mood. The present tense means it is to be a continuous happening. That is to say, you must continually be filled with the Spirit. The imperative means that it is a command. We are commanded to be filled with the Spirit. This places a responsibility on us for yieldedness and for obedience.

Being filled with the Spirit presupposes a personal experience with the Holy Spirit. It is, of course, the Spirit who fills us. What then is it that we do? It is important to recognize what we are to do and what God will do. We repent, he forgives; we confess Christ, he accepts us. We commit our lives to Jesus as Lord, he justifies and baptizes with the Spirit. We yield ourselves and then he fills us. As one obeys, he then controls. In one sense we are just as filled with the Spirit as we are emptied of self. We are just as filled with the Spirit as we want to be. In Acts 5:32 we read, "We are witnesses of those things, and so is the Holy Spirit, whom God has given to those who obey him." The Holy Spirit has come to be in control of one's life, but for his control we must give ourselves in obedience.

The Holy Spirit filling one's life means that we are free from other powers because he is here. As you step into a room that is in darkness and you turn on the light, the light expels the darkness. Likewise, when the Spirit of God moves into one's life, his presence expels things that are contrary to the Spirit of God. One can get rid of bitterness, negativism, hypercriticism by opening one's self to the Holy Spirit and letting him move in. To get rid of the problem of jealousy or envy one must open his life to the Holy Spirit and let him come in with his love. Where love is present, it "covers over a multitude of sins," including the tendency to sin and to live selfishly. So the Spirit-filled life is the power to overcome or transcend the drives of the self. Paul says, "Live by the Spirit and you will not gratify the desires [or drives] of the self" (Ephesians 5:16). This is a very clear promise. We can claim it and live his way. This is his liberating power.

But we cannot be filled with the Spirit unless we are daily involved with him, unless we individually and personally open our lives to the Holy Spirit. While the Holy Spirit is at work in the church and in the world, he does his work through us. We share in the work of the Spirit in a personal way as we open ourselves to him. We are now doing business with a personal God who mediates his presence in our lives by the Holy Spirit. We should pray day by day, "Lord, fill me with your Spirit for today." We can then walk with him, practicing the presence of God. And as we daily acknowledge the Spirit's presence, we won't quench him, we won't grieve him, nor will we resist his leading. This leading is always focused on the will of Christ. The Spirit has come to glorify Christ, and as we live to glorify Christ the Holy Spirit will fill our lives. Where Jesus Christ is glorified there the Spirit is in his fullness.

Being filled with the Spirit provides personal power from the Holy Spirit.

In saying, "individual power," we are recognizing that there is no code or formula that is the same for all of us in terms of our personal makeup. With respect to our temperaments, we are all affected differently due to the psychological aspects of our makeup, and our different intellectual dimensions and approaches. It is important that we recognize the particularity of our temperaments. I must understand my problems, my drives, my impatience, my ambitions; and all of this needs to be brought under the control of the Holy Spirit.

We must avoid seeking to copy some other person's experience of being filled with the Spirit. Let that person radiate all of the joy and freedom that God gives him. Don't be jealous of him. But neither should we copy him. Each of us must be certain that we are facing our own nature and dealing with our temperaments honestly and bringing the total self under the lordship of Christ. The Spirit gives to "each one, just as he determines" (1 Corinthians 12:11).

The Spirit has the ability to permeate the total personality, the mind and subconscious, the emotions and the will. When he takes possession of the subconscious mind he cleanses and redirects it. E. Stanley Jones speaks of the three psychological and physiological urges which the Spirit transforms: the self urge, the sex urge, and the social or herd urge. "Those urges are still there, for the person is not depersonalized. The self is there, but no longer at the center, no longer controlling life. The self is a Spirit-controlled self. The life is not sex-controlled, but Spirit-controlled. The herd urge is still there, but no longer fastened on such entities as class, or race, or nation as supreme loyalties. Now it is fastened on the kingdom of God as the supreme loyalty, and all other loyalties are subsidiary to that absolute loyalty." °

This is an important insight on the broader implications of the power of the Spirit. We too often think of the Spirit in primarily pietistic and mystical terms rather than social and ethical terms. His power enables us to behave differently, to be Christlike in life patterns as well as spirit or attitudes. The active nature of faith calls us to live out our beliefs.

Being filled with the Spirit requires personal obedience to the Holy Spirit.

God gives the Holy Spirit "to those who obey him" (Acts 5:32). No one else can obey for you. No one else yields for you. No one else surrenders for you. But Christians have at

---

° *Ibid*, p. 276.

times overplayed the word "surrender," to the point of missing the meaning of obedience. I have counseled people who said, "I have yielded and yielded and what do I do now?" Well, it is time to act in faith; it is time to take the initiative and move. By obeying you will discover that God is right there, moving with you. It is time to act on the basis of obedience.

Paul's expression in Ephesians 5:18 is in the present tense, meaning we are to continually be filled with the Holy Spirit. We don't talk about being filled as though this is a static experience, but we are continually to be filled. It is commanded—we must be filled with the Spirit! This means living with an attitude of obedience, the desire to walk in his will, to be controlled by him.

Again, this doesn't mean that one has all of the Holy Spirit, it means that the Holy Spirit is to have all of us. This is an important awareness. If you dip a bottle into the ocean until the bottle is filled, you have the ocean in the bottle but you don't have all of the ocean in the bottle! And so it is with the Holy Spirit. He is so great that we do not talk about how we got him, or how we get all of him, or any language of that type. We talk about yielding ourselves so that he can have all of us. And this is the meaning of being filled with the Spirit. It isn't how much of the Holy Spirit we have, it is how much of us the Holy Spirit has. And this is simply other language for the emphasis in Christian faith on yieldedness to the lordship of Jesus Christ. As we yield ourselves to his lordship he becomes master in life by the person and presence of the Holy Spirit.

Faith is living with an attitude of openness to God, that you are moving with him in your life. My friend Bill Pannell has defined faith as "the attitude which permits God to be himself in one's life." Individual obedience to the Holy

Spirit allows the Holy Spirit to do his work in one's life. But in emphasizing a personal experience we should beware of individualism. God does not destroy our *individuality*, our personal uniqueness, but he does free us from *individualism*. In obedience to the Spirit we are a part of the body of Christ, of a community of believers. It is in the partnership of a brotherhood that the Spirit enriches our individual lives through the many gifts he is releasing in the group. Obedience to the Spirit means living in freedom among others who are sharing the fellowship of the Spirit.

In his book, *Love Within Limits*, a commentary on 1 Corinthians 13, Lewis B. Smedes speaks of "collegial power" as love functioning in community, ministering to each other's strengths. This collegial power, he says, is "edifying power, the power to build, to nurture, to add to the strengths of persons." The experience of community or brotherhood is not a "leveler" in the sense of making us all the same. In the truly Christian experience of community we respect the various gifts of the Spirit which vary from person to person and thereby enrich the whole. Any attempt to destroy the uniqueness of persons, to conform them to a "sameness" in the group, is more likely motivated by selfishness and envy rather than by love and brotherhood. The parable of the talents reveals that God expects each person to be faithful in the use of the opportunities presented to him (Luke 19:11-27). It is especially clear in the parable that God's commendation is not in relation to the number of opportunities but is for faithful use of those which come to us. The community of believers should be a support fellowship, an enabling group which liberates persons for effective service.

It is the liberating fellowship that gives evidence that we "look not only to [our] ... own interests, but also to the interests of others" (Philippians 2:4). We are a part of the body of Christ, the one body into which the Spirit has inducted us. The greater evidence of our obedience in the Spirit is our participation in the fellowship of disciples. Individualistic patterns are evidence that we are failing to enjoy fully the sense of belonging in the body of Christ. This is answered by yielding to the will of the Spirit.

There is a poem which sums up this matter of yieldedness and openness to the fullness of the Spirit.

> Oh, the bitter pain and sorrow,
>   That a time could ever be,
> When I proudly said to Jesus,
>   "All of self and none of thee."
>
> Yet he found me, I beheld him
>   Bleeding on the accursed tree,
> And my wistful heart said faintly,
>   "Some of self and some of thee."
>
> Day by day his tender mercy,
>   Healing, helping, full and free,
> Brought me lower while I whispered,
>   "Less of self and more of thee."
>
> Higher than the highest heaven,
>   Deeper than the deepest sea,
> Lord, thy love at last has conquered,
>   "None of self and all of thee."

Prayer:

> Father God, in the name of the Lord Jesus,
> we pray that you will help each of us who
> have thought on this theme to be emptied
> of self and open to the Holy Spirit, so
> that we might know his fullness, his con-
> trol, that it may be none of self and all
> of thee. Glorify Christ through us and
> teach us how to walk in obedience to the
> Word in the Spirit.
>
>   Amen.

Study Questions

1. How does the revelation of God in Christ affect our understanding of the Holy Spirit?

2. How do we relate the Spirit-filled life or sanctification to justification by faith?

3. How can we rediscover the meaning of community in our social structures in society?

4. How can membership in the body of Christ be expressed in our priorities in life in our twentieth-century lifestyle?

7
THE GIFTS OF THE HOLY SPIRIT

7

The Gifts of the Holy Spirit

> Now there are varieties of gifts, but the same Spirit; and
> there are varieties of service, but the same Lord; and there are
> varieties of working, but the same God who inspires them all
> in everyone. To each is given the manifestations of the Spirit
> for the common good. To one is given through the Spirit the
> utterance of wisdom, to another the utterance of knowledge
> according to the same Spirit, to another faith by the same
> Spirit, to another gifts of healing by the one Spirit, to another
> the ability to distinguish between spirits, to another various
> kinds of tongues, to another the interpretation of tongues. All
> these are inspired by one and the same Spirit, who apportions
> to each one individually as he wills.
>
> *1 Corinthians 12:4-11, author's translation.*

Someone has said if the religion of China is Confucianism,
the religion of America is confusion. You may have heard of
the man who dashed into a bookstore and said, "Have you
got that book, *A Piece of My Mind*, by Rabbi Norman
Vincent Sheen?" There are many people this confused
about life who don't know where to turn for an answer.
Similarly, many people are confused about the gifts of the
Holy Spirit and are seeking answers.

This study on the person and work of the Holy Spirit now

brings us to a focus on the gifts of the Holy Spirit. We have been studying the *gift* of the Spirit, that is Christ gives the Holy Spirit, Christ baptizes with the Spirit so that the Spirit is present in our lives. We have also been emphasizing that one must obey the Spirit, walk in the Spirit, be filled with the Spirit so that we might know what it is to live in the Spirit or be led by the Spirit. From the numerous terms in the New Testament about the work of the Spirit we have been focusing especially upon knowing the person of the Spirit himself.

In this section we will emphasize the gifts of the Spirit, and will focus later on the fruit of the Spirit, our interpretation of the gifts of the Spirit is from the perspective of a basic biblicism. With our dependence on the Spirit we could entitle this chapter, "Enabled Persons." We need new persons for these times who know what it is to be enlightened by the Word of God through the illumination of the Spirit, and enabled by his ability to do God's will. The text used in this section, 1 Corinthians 12 to 14, could be outlined with three points: (1) the gifts of grace enable the body of Christ (ch. 12), (2) the gift of love enriches the body (ch. 13), (3) the gift of prophecy edifies the body (ch. 14).

This enabling of the body of Christ may be expressed in various ways, but it is done by his power. It was my privilege to share in Indonesia with congregations made alive through revival awakening, but their expression of the gifts of the Spirit was not with the emphasis so prominent in the Western charismatic movement. Rather I was told, "We don't speak much about the Holy Spirit, we just glorify Christ, and the Holy Spirit does his work." Very soon afterward I was in Taiwan in mission workers' conferences. Here there is an unusual movement of the Spirit among the Tayal mountain people, with unusual happenings of "discernment" by the Holy Spirit. Emphasizing the gift of discernment, they reject tongues as though from a demonic source. Paul's admonition to "eagerly desire the greater gifts" (1 Corinthians 12:31) may mean that we should seek the best gift of the Spirit for a particular need or work. This excludes any emphasis on one gift as the uniform evidence of the presence of the Spirit. (We will note an alternate reading of this passage later in this chapter.)

Though we are now focusing upon 1 Corinthians 12, chapters 12 to 14 is the context in which the apostle Paul is answering problems which arose from the individualistic way in which different persons expressed their gifts. One of the problems in the Corinthian church was boastfulness about their many gifts. Paul reminds them that gifts in themselves are not evidence of spirituality. He reminds them they lack no gift (1 Corinthians 1:7), yet they are carnal (1 Corinthians 3:1). Gifts from the Spirit are not in themselves evidence of spirituality. One may be carnal and still have certain gifts which the Holy Spirit has given for the larger purpose of the Spirit's work in the church. Notice in the passage that gifts are given to each person in the congregation. We need to recognize these gifts and respect what God wants to do with different abilities and personalities in the church.

Paul also states that the Spirit's gifts are given for the common good. Gifts are not given to exalt some individual. They are not spiritual status symbols. One should not flaunt some particular gift that the Holy Spirit is giving him. If he has given us a gift to teach, or a gift of wisdom, we should not become arrogant as though we stand above others. If he has given us the gift of preaching so that we can preach with clarity, love, and eloquence, we should not act as though, because of the gift, we are above other persons. If he has given other gifts of ministry, they should not be used to gain personal advantages. In this passage Paul is calling us to an honest awareness of what these gifts mean. His gifts enrich but do not replace the calling to serve others.

Of course, the greatest gift of all is the *gift from Christ of the Spirit himself!* From the Spirit there is the *gift of Christ-likeness* (Romans 8:29; Galatians 5:22-25). With this is the *gift of Christians* to each other in Christian community. When the Holy Spirit converts someone with his or her potential, abilities, and gifts, he gives the church a new gift in the person he has converted. And *community itself is a gift of the Spirit*, it is a healing, affirming, liberating fellowship.

In fact, the greater thing the Holy Spirit is doing is in creating a new community, a new people of God. On the day of Pentecost the greater thing that happened was not the miraculous signs. It was not the sound of a rushing mighty wind, a symbol of *inspiration.* Nor was it the tongues of fire over the heads of the group, a symbol of *purification* that his presence is now in each person who names Christ as Lord. Nor was it the gift of languages, the symbol of *communication*, a sign which demonstrated that the gospel is not simply for one people but for all people. As mentioned previously Paul quotes a passage from Isaiah 28:11 to show that the gift of languages at Pentecost was a fulfillment of Scripture: "With foreign lips and strange tongues God speaks to this people" (1 Corinthians 14:21). Here is evidence that the gospel is for all nations and all tongues. But the greater thing on the day of Pentecost, beyond these three miraculous signs, was and is the new community which the Holy Spirit began creating. This new brotherhood, this new covenant community, the actual experience of community, is a gift of the Spirit.

For the equipping of this new community, the Spirit gives

gifts of edification or enrichment. In addition to the passage introducing this chapter, there are references to gifts in Ephesians 4, Romans 12, and 1 Corinthians 14. A. W. Tozer, of the Christian Missionary Alliance Church, tabulated at least eighteen gifts of the Spirit, not just nine of them. When people talk about the nine gifts of the Spirit, they are too limited, for there are many gifts. In fact, the Holy Spirit can create some new gifts, if he needs them, in meeting the problems of a modern age. God isn't some "old fogey" who can't keep up with this hot-rodding, teenage generation! God is active, creative; in fact, he is continually creating (John 5:17), and through the Holy Spirit he is creating a new people.

There are also *gifts of extension*. These are gifts of insight, of unction, and of boldness to witness. His gifts extend the ministry of the church to outreach in society and the world. As we reflect on 1 Corinthians 12:7-10, we can recognize a fellowship role for gifts in the church, but also an equipping role for mission. Gifts of wisdom, knowledge, faith, healing, and prophecy all contribute to the extension of the kingdom of Christ in society. In fact, gifts such as teaching, helping, giving, administration, and counseling are all important factors in the servant role of the church in mission. When the gift becomes an end in itself it becomes an encumbrance in the servant mission of the church.

There are different concepts regarding the actual presence of gifts of the Spirit. Some say that the gifts of the Spirit were limited to the first century. But this position is hardly consistent, because those holding this position tend to select certain of the gifts and say that they were limited to the first century as signs of the risen Christ, and regard other gifts as proper to be expressed in the church today. This is not the answer to the problem of phenomenal gifts—

expressions which are different from what one might think of as the normal way the Spirit of God uses the powers and expressions of human personality. It is better for us to affirm the statement of the Scripture that he gives gifts "according to his own will" (Hebrews 2:4, KJV).

The gifts of the Spirit are not limited to time; they are limited to God's purpose. He gives gifts so that they can glorify Jesus Christ. His gifts are not something which we manipulate or induce. Whenever one feels that he has powers through some human manipulation, they are no doubt psychic powers, similar to the power the occult uses. But spiritual gifts or powers are gifts from the Holy Spirit. And when the Holy Spirit gives his gifts he gives them without human manipulation. As we pray and trust the Holy Spirit, he will give gifts according to his will.

The Spirit's work of glorifying Christ is evident in his administration of gifts, as well as in other aspects of discipleship. Gifts of healing, discernment, and even of exorcising demons, often accompany the frontiers of revival and evangelism. When the Spirit breaks into new areas of religion and culture his work is often accompanied by healings and exorcisms. While this may not be the norm for mature Christian fellowships, it is not abnormal in the mission of Christ in cutting new ground with the gospel.

As to the particular gift of tongues, there are many people who are experiencing a happening of glossolalia as a special phenomenon in our time. My own conviction is that since our times are very experience- and sensory-oriented, to meet people today God has been almost forced to come through in more experiential and sensory ways. I do not believe that these particular gifts are evidence of greater spirituality today than our fathers had. Rather, I believe they are an evidence of the Holy Spirit meeting people wherever they are and giving different gifts at different times because of where he finds people.

While I have received gifts of the Spirit, and he has given me a certain discernment, insight, and ability to preach and share the gospel, he has not given me a gift of tongues. I have honestly prayed about this. I believe that if one is not open to tongues he is not consecrated, but if one begins demanding tongues he is not consecrated either! This would be telling the Spirit what gifts to give us. And so to my brothers and sisters who speak in tongues, I must say, don't demand this of everyone and be careful that you practice this only as the Spirit directs in the understanding of Jesus Christ. In this way, the Word becomes the authority. And to persons who know the fullness of the Holy Spirit and have not experienced tongues, I must also say, don't feel inferior about your experience, for the presence of the Holy Spirit isn't measured by one particular gift. No one gift becomes the proof that one has experienced the Spirit.

But human nature is such that we like to have proof. I have found this through the years in evangelistic preaching. Many people want a feeling-proof for assurance of salvation. This problem is very common, for some people find it difficult to take Christ at his Word by faith. They want a feeling-proof that they are saved. In a similar way with respect to the Holy Spirit, there are many people who want some gift-proof that they have received the Holy Spirit.

A pastor friend from England says that his experience in glossolalia was first a power for him, and then a problem. He had to ask the Lord to take this away because he was using it as the symbol that he was spiritual in his work in the church. In fact, he found himself relying on this, and when he missed out on refurbishing his own spirit in prayer and Bible study he would turn to this gift of tongues as a guarantee that he was still spiritual! And suddenly he discovered that his soul was shrinking. Can we be that honest?

In reading the spiritual autobiography of E. Stanley Jones, I was impressed with his remarkable testimony of the infilling of the Spirit. "Wave after wave of the Spirit seemed to be going through me as a cleansing fire. I could only walk the floor with tears of joy flowing down my cheeks. I could do nothing but praise him—and did. I know this was no passing emotion; the Holy Spirit had come to abide with me forever." Following a discussion on the manifestation of tongues, Jones says, "I'm grateful that I receive the Holy Spirit without complications or riders. The Holy Spirit brought me purity and he brought me power, for he brought me himself. I need and want no more." ° And this is where I am as well, enjoying his presence.

Interpreting the several occasions of "Pentecostal phenomena" in the book of Acts, I have frequently pointed out that these were God's confirmation of creating His people from all nationalities. In Acts 2 it was a Jewish Pentecost; in Acts 8, a Samaritan Pentecost; in Acts 11, a Gentile Pentecost; and in Acts 19, a Greek Pentecost. E. Stanley Jones interprets these occasions similarly. Following the inscription on the cross, "This is Jesus, the King of the Jews" (Matthew 27:37), written in Hebrew, Latin, and Greek, he said the various happenings of Pentecost languages which needed no interpreter were extending this universal claim. "It is true that in the Acts the gift of tongues was associated with the coming of the Holy Spirit in three places— Jerusalem, Caesarea and Ephesus; the centers of Hebrew culture, Roman culture and Greek culture. The question was very acute in those early days as to whether if you became a

---

° *Ibid.*, pp. 53, 59.

Christian you would also have to adopt the Hebrew culture and language, become a Jew. The pattern was broken at Pentecost."[°]

One who truly knows the sovereign presence of the Holy Spirit will be humble about the work of the Spirit. If the Spirit gives particular gifts, we will use them for the glory of Christ. We should never use them as status symbols. We should never become divisive in the church with a "we—they" language. We should not judge other persons by saying that, unless they have a particular gift, they aren't as spiritual as we are.

Paul says, "You are the body of Christ, and each one of you is a part of it. And in the church God has appointed, first of all, apostles, second, prophets, third, teachers, then workers of miracles, also those having gifts of healing, those able to help others, those with gifts of administration, and those speaking in different kinds of tongues" (1 Corinthians 12:27, 28). There now follows a series of rhetorical questions: "Are all apostles?" (The answer is no.) "Are all prophets?" (The answer is no.) "Are all teachers?" (The answer is no.) "Do all work miracles?" (The expected answer is no.) "Do all have gifts of healing?" (The answer is no.) "Do all speak in tongues?" (The answer is no.) "Do all interpret?" (The answer is no.) Paul's word is, "But eagerly desire the greater gifts. And now I will show you the most excellent way. If I speak in the tongues of men and of angels, but have not love, I am only a resounding gong or a clanging cymbal" (12:29—13:1). Paul then presents the most sublime passage in literature, a poem of love as the ultimate expression that one is Christlike.

In exegeting 1 Corinthians 12:31, it is important to note

[°] *Ibid.*, p. 57.

that the Greek leaves us without certainty on how it is to be rendered. Some verb forms in the Greek are identical for both the present indicative and for the imperative. The King James Version translates the phrase as imperative—"covet earnestly the best gifts"—saying thereby that we are to be always seeking the better gifts. However, the same Greek word can be present indicative, which would be translated, "You Corinthians are always seeking the best gifts." This translation makes the statement into a matter-of-fact understanding of a characteristic of the Corinthian church which is obsessed with a search for the more spectacular gifts. This latter interpretation seems to me to be the more likely in the context, and emphasizes Paul's next thrust, "Let me show you a more excellent way!" At least it follows that in chapter 13 Paul elevates the practice of love above the performance of gifts.

To conclude this chapter here are several summary observations:

First, the Spirit's gifts are his endowments for maximizing the potential of any person. The Spirit wants to use us to the full in building the kingdom of Christ. In Christ he has made us new creatures (2 Corinthians 5:17), the creative Spirit being the agent of this renewal. He equips us, giving us the power to become all that we should be as children of God.

Second, the Spirit's gifts are given according to his will (Hebrews 2:4), not simply according to our desires. When the Scripture says "covet earnestly the best gifts," it isn't putting a hierarchy on these gifts. Rather it is calling us to seek that which is God's best for us in his work in a given situation. In another situation we may well need a different gift for his work.

Third, the gifts are given to the church for the perfecting

of the brotherhood. They are not given for individualistic achievement but for the common good (1 Corinthians 12:7). The word "edification" is prominent in Paul's discussion, as is the word "exhortation." But in addition he mentions gifts of wisdom, administration, and management. The Spirit enriches the community of disciples through the gifts among the disciples.

Fourth, the Spirit's gifts are not status symbols, they are service potentials. We are a part of the larger service of the church. Unfortunately, church organizations have generally used the "democratic process" of voting rather than to have a gift discernment process. In an election a good person always loses, and waits a term before opportunity to be considered again. If the congregation functioned by discerning gifts we could better seek ways to involve each person in a service for which they are gifted. However, the ideal is to move beyond "filling offices" needed for the life of the group, to maximizing the full potential of the community of faith. This means engaging the laity in the work of ministering for Christ in the larger community according to the gifts of each person.

Finally, the Spirit's gifts never become more important than the giver. Whenever we place more attention on the gifts than on the giver himself, we have already failed. It is the Holy Spirit who is the ultimate gift. Worship is the joy of reverence in his presence, a spirit too often lacking in our services. Dr. Samuel Miller has said, "To worship God and be less shaken than when one views the movie, "Dr. Zhivago," or less involved than when one reads Kafka's *Trial*, is a strange commentary on the superficiality of our religious habits!"

The Holy Spirit is God present, the supreme experience. The gift of the Holy Spirit comes to us in different expressions, like gift packages with different wrappings, and yet we pay so much attention to the wrapping and minimize the gift himself. Imagine receiving a Christmas present and sitting there admiring the wrapping and the ribbon and not opening the present! The Holy Spirit is the gift. The manifestations are like the wrapping. It is his presence that is important for the glory of Jesus Christ.

> Father God, forgive us where we have
> used our gifts in ways which made them
> prominent because they were important to
> us and to our advancement. Help us to
> more conscientiously surrender to the
> glory of Christ and the freedom of the
> Spirit, your greater gift. Through
> Christ, our Lord. Amen.

Study Questions

1. What meaning does the community of disciples have in our lives for the discernment and encouragement of the use of our gifts?

2. In what sense can the community of disciples pray for gifts of the Spirit needed in their fellowship but not evident among them?

3. How can we encourage persons who have some of the less spectacular gifts, such as intercessory prayer, to be aware of our appreciation and support for their role?

4. How can we better discern the gifts of the Spirit in our fellowship to maximize his ministry among us?

8
THE FRUIT OF THE HOLY SPIRIT

8

The Fruit of the Holy Spirit

So I say, live by the Spirit, and you will not gratify the desires of the sinful nature. For the sinful nature desires what is contrary to the Spirit, and the Spirit what is contrary to the sinful nature. They are in conflict with each other, so that you do not do what you want. But if you are led by the Spirit, you are not under law.

The acts of the sinful nature are obvious: sexual immorality, impurity and debauchery; idolatry and witchcraft; hatred, discord, jealousy, fits of rage, selfish ambition, dissensions, factions and envy; drunkenness, orgies, and the like. I warn you, as I did before, that those who live like this will not inherit the kingdom of God.

Galatians 5:16-26.

Eric Routley says, "There are three dimensions to one's Christian life that must always be faced. The first, where the will of God is done. The second, where the will of God is rejected. And the third, where redemption is in process." For most of us, if not all, there are some areas where the will of God is done. We have done it and we rejoice in it. There are some areas on which we need to be convicted, for the will of God was rejected by our decision and we took the lesser route. But most important is the dimension in which redemption is in process.

When one walks in the Spirit, he has the confidence that he is walking in a divine process. That is, God is in the process of changing our lives into the image of Christ. And change is one of the most exciting things about life. In Christian discipleship we are growing in the ability to live. Many need to discover that Christian living is a joyous, satisfying, meaningful life here and now.

We have one vocation in this life, that of being a disciple of Christ. This vocation is primary, our occupations are not. An individual's purpose is more important than his or her position, and our purpose is to be disciples. Since we don't know what occupational changes we will be facing in the next ten years, the more important thing is being prepared to live. The Spirit is constantly educating us for life, and a major part of our life is social and spiritual. This means that we need to understand God and his will, learn to live in obedience to his Word, to think his thoughts, and to walk in the Spirit. Discipling others means helping them to develop as whole persons, to know the fruit of the Spirit in life and to express wholeness in love, joy, and peace—expressions of the fruit of the Spirit.

In the passage we are studying from Galatians 5, there is a contrast between the works of the flesh and the fruit of the Spirit. One could wish to make adjectives out of these words. This would be to say, "The fruit of the Spirit is love—joyous, peaceful, patient, kind, good, faithful, gentle, self-controlling love." It is really love that enables one to express all of these characteristics. However, to make these words adjectives would let us talk simply about love as a personal category, and divorce it from the person of the Holy Spirit who gives this fruit. It is the Spirit, not love, which is making everything that is listed here happen. True, love is the oil on the cogs of the wheels of life, love makes the wheels turn smoothly. In the Christian experience to know God is to know love, for "whoever does not love does not know God because God is love," but "everyone who loves has been born of God and knows God" (1 John 4:7, 8).

Yet the question is, How do we achieve love? Where do we get the power to love? The answer of Scripture is that love is not something you work up by your own ability, love is experienced in relationship with another. And that other is God who is known in Christ and mediated to us by the Holy Spirit. Paul said, "God has poured out his love into our hearts by the Holy Spirit, whom he has given us" (Romans 5:5). This is where we get the power to love the unlovely when we don't have it or the power to be patient when we don't have it. The answer of the Christian gospel is to open yourself to the Holy Spirit and pray simply, "You be my love."

The classic passage on love is 1 Corinthians 13. There are several very searching expressions about love in these beautiful lines. "Love never fails. Love is never envious. Love never keeps a record. Love is never bitter. Love is never uptight. Love is not critical." And love covers a multitude of sins, that is, it covers over or keeps us from sinning. In Galatians 5 love is a fruit of the Spirit.

The fruit of the Spirit is experienced by a conscious abiding in the Holy Spirit.

In John 15, Jesus said, "Abide in me, and I in you. As the branch cannot bear fruit by itself, unless it abides in the vine, neither can you unless you abide in me" (John 15:4, RSV). In the chapter preceding, and in the one following, Jesus speaks of the coming of the Holy Spirit. He said, "On that day you will realize that I am in my Father, and you are in me, and I am in you" (John 14:20). Predicting the coming

111

of the Holy Spirit, Jesus said that when he would come the world would not understand him, but the disciples would know him, for he would be with and within the disciple. Jesus said, "He lives with you and will be in you" (John 14:17). He is referring to his presence in the person of the Holy Spirit. This means that we understand the fruit of the Spirit as an expression of the Spirit's life within us.

To use Jesus' illustration, the life one expects from the branch is the same life that is in the vine. And the character of the fruit on the branch is determined by the vine. This is to say that the vine has the life. If you graft a branch into the vine of a different plant, the fruit would still be dependent on the vine. The Spirit of God comes into lives that are branches of the vine, Christ, and the new fruit that comes forth is the fruit of the vine. God is doing something in our experience which affirms this as the fruit of the Spirit. This is seen in contrast to the deeds of the flesh. This new process means that the Spirit replaces the old expressions of the flesh with the fruit of the Spirit. When Paul says, "Live by the Spirit, and you will not gratify the desires of the sinful nature" (Galatians 5:16), he is saying the expressions of your life are now to be true to the presence of the Spirit because the life of the Spirit is flowing through you.

The fruit of the Spirit is the expression of the Spirit himself.

The Spirit can enrich and change our personalities and our dispositions. It is significant that this list of the fruit of the Spirit is personality-oriented. Seven of the nine deal specifically with our relationships. These expressions are mainly aspects of what we call personality disposition. There are nine expressions, like nine slices of a Valencia orange. It is one fruit and yet you can pull off one slice after another. Just so, in the fruit of the Spirit there are nine facets.

The first is love which means *sharing to enrich others*. This is agape love—divine love, sharing to enrich. No matter what the cost is to one's self we are interested in enriching another. Human love (phileo), in contrast, is love that depends upon the attractiveness of another or depends upon mutual benefits. But agape love does not depend on what we receive from another, it is sharing to enrich. It is relating to another for the enrichment of his or her experience.

Joy is *the feeling of love*, it is delight in God. Joy is harmony of spirit. But joy is not the same as pleasure. You get pleasure out of things—hobbies, for instance—but you get joy out of relationships. Whenever something is wrong in the relationship between you and the person that is important in your life, your joy is gone. You may still have pleasure in some things, but there is no joy, life is empty. Joy is harmony of spirit, it is delight in God.

Peace is *the practice of love*. Peace means the absence of disturbing factors, the removal of hostility. Peace is positive, active, for pursuing peace is to live in love, to practice love. "If it is possible, as far as it depends upon you, live at peace with everyone" (Romans 12:18). When we know the love of the Spirit, there is more power lying within us than we often exercise! By his power we have the possibility of living at peace with others, and of being peacemakers.

Patience is *the preservation of love*. Patience means one believes so strongly in what God is doing in the victory of the Spirit that as a consequence one can be patient in a given situation while discerning what God is working out. When we become impatient, when we retaliate, or when we speak back with raised voice and harsh words seeking to dominate the conversation, impatience destroys the fruit of the Spirit. Anger, enmity, and hostility are expressions of the flesh.

Kindness is *the expression of love*. Love is always kind, as

Paul writes in 1 Corinthians 13, always tender toward other persons. Love doesn't violate another personality, it doesn't manipulate or misuse persons. It expresses the courtesy which says to another, "You are important." And God has said this to us, for "the kindness and love of God our Saviour appeared" (Titus 3:4). God accepts us in spite of what we have done. God is not uptight about our sins. He moves beyond the issue to the person. God, in his kindness, cares more about us than about what we have done. As Lewis Smedes says of kindness that serves, "servant power is personal power used to increase the power of a weaker person."°

Goodness is *the action of love.* Love acts in good deeds, love takes the initiative, love acts on behalf of another. Goodness is the expression which demonstrates to another that he or she is important. The servant role means that one takes the initiative to serve others. Goodness also demonstrates the graciousness of one's life. To be gracious toward another, to do deeds of goodness, means that we are committed to enriching life by enriching persons. What an answer to the tensions of our society. What an answer to the problems between the haves and the have nots. Service requires mutual respect. Goodness is the action of love.

Next is faithfulness, *the loyalty of love.* In a message by Dr. Paul Scherer on the relation between law and love, he said, "There is law in love and love in law." There is love in law—ask any parent—for there is love in the commandments and discipline. But there is also law in love—ask any married couple—because there is the law of fidelity. Faithfulness is loyalty. When we talk about faith toward God we

---

°Lewis B. Smedes, *Love Within Limits* (Grand Rapids: Eerdmans, 1978), p. 12.

need this dimension of integrity, of loyalty, of faithfulness. It is the loyalty of love.

And gentleness is *the attitude of love*. This has to do with meekness. But meekness is not weakness. Meekness is strength, because it means one has the inner control to be gentle, to be gracious. Such people esteem others as more important than what is happening to themselves. One who serves in the spirit of Christ does not seek compensation or recognition. Serving others means to relinquish power for the sake of a relationship of redemptive influence.

Finally, self-control is *the restraint of love*. Self-control enables us to bring our better selves to others. There is vulnerability in service. We lay ourselves open to the hurts and pains of relationships. But when we practice self-control, instead of hurting another by our frustrations and tensions by pouring out our angers, we resolve those angers in love and relate with the wholeness and openness that enriches both lives. Patience is the ultimate restraint.

When I think of God's sovereignty I do not think of sovereignty as some kind of authoritarianism in which God determines everything in the lives of all creation under him. Rather, he permits us freedom. Sovereignty is best expressed in God's patience. God is sovereign in that he has control within himself. He does not break in upon us with judgments of wrath, but he keeps working in love to redeem and to change us. This is why he says, "Vengeance is *mine*." He is the only one who can control and temper it with mercy and justice.

The fruit of the Spirit is the existential sense of freedom "to be."

He frees us, enabling us to behave our beliefs. But he does this by adding to belief and behavior the third basic element of being. Paul says, "The law of the Spirit of life in Christ Jesus has set me free from the law of sin and death" (Romans 8:2). This is the power of a positive faith, of a freedom to be. One finds his self-identity in faith, in his freedom from self-centeredness. The law of the Spirit of life supersedes the law of sin, a freedom which we enjoy as we understand the laws of the spiritual life.

The "law of love" gives us freedom to be free! We need not be dominated by angers, resentment, self-will, prejudice, or critical attitudes. Each of us has angers, for anger is the reaction of a concerned self when things don't move the way we would like. But the law of love enables us to understand and redirect the energies of anger rather than to let them smolder in resentment. The law of love also enables us to avoid venting anger upon persons while we are angry about issues. The energy of anger can be directed into creative acts which can now cope with problems. The concerns that give rise to anger can be recycled in creative love!

The "law of faith" can release us from fear, worry, nervousness, and anxiety. Since these problems arise from our awareness that we can't control everything in our experience, there is power for us to be composed and trusting amidst experiences not fully determined by us. In a very real sense worry or anxiety is a result of one's pride. Most of us have been conditioned to master the happenings in our lives; when we face something we can't master, we are frustrated. Worry is an ego frustrated by its own limitations. Once we admit our limitations and acknowledge the presence of God and his providence to care for things beyond us, we have an answer to our anxiety. Only then can we truly quote Romans 8:28: "In all things God works for the good of those who love him, who have been called according to his purpose."

The "law of peace" answers the problems of guilt, greed, lust, and intemperance which beset us. Peace is an active harmony in one's life. When one has made peace with God and his conscience, he can be at ease in his own personality. A guilty person is never a good participant in life; he can't enjoy life because he is always obsessed with his own guilt. Even service motivated by guilt is a perversion, a compensation. If one will but confess his guilt this will break its tyranny and he will be free. Peace is the answer to the inner drive of greed, or lust, or intemperance, for one defeated by these is being driven by inner problems or insecurities. We should beware of seeking to satisfy the insecurities we have over status, or sexuality, or self-fulfillment without resolving the more basic issue of who we are as persons. Peace comes when each person made in the image of God is in harmony with the true self in the grace of God.

One may also speak of the "law of joy." Paul says, "The kingdom of God is not a matter of eating and drinking, but of righteousness, peace and joy in the Holy Spirit" (Romans 14:17). Joy is the pleasure of right relationships. It is not simply pleasure, for you can get pleasure out of things, but joy comes from relationships. And joy is his answer to the problems of fluctuating moods, negativism, or pouting. We often have personal grief over loss, over loss of goods, of position, or over some injustice. We have been hurt, and consequently become negative or bitter. The experience of joy elevates our relationship with Christ and the people of God above our losses. Joy has the power for healing, power to release us from pouting, power to draw us out of ourselves in fellowship.

At rest in him, we can know the inner security of the Spirit of God at work in us. We can trust him to bring to us each day those qualities which will enhance our maturity in grace.

117

"He who began a good work in you will carry it on to completion until the day of Jesus Christ" (Philippians 1:6). The fruit is the fruit of the Spirit, we are only the bearers in which he conveys the life that produces fruit.

> Spirit of God, we are asking through
> Jesus our Lord that you would mediate
> to each of us the dynamic of your
> presence so that your fruit may be
> seen in our lives, to the glory of
> Christ.   Amen.

Study Questions

1. To what degree does the Spirit use our relationships with others to help us recognize and develop in the fruit of the Spirit?

2. How can love become a lifestyle for the believer when our orientation is self-centeredness?

3. How do we relate maturing in grace to the gifts of the Spirit?

4. To what extent can we distinguish love as an ethical norm rather than simply a mystical or pietistic feeling?

5. How does love build bridges across social or cultural difference?

9
SEALED WITH THE HOLY SPIRIT OF CHRIST

9

Sealed with the Holy
Spirit of Christ

> Now it is God who makes both us and you stand firm in
> Christ. He anointed us, set his seal of ownership on us, and
> put his Spirit in our hearts as a deposit, guaranteeing what is
> to come. *2 Corinthians 1:21, 22*

> In him you also, who have heard the word of truth, the gospel
> of your salvation, and have believed in him, were sealed with
> the promised Holy Spirit.
> *Ephesians 1:13, author's translation.*

If you live your faith by your own power your faith isn't
big enough. Faith in Jesus Christ introduces us to a life beyond our own abilities. This is the grace of God in the power
of his Holy Spirit freeing us to live differently. This is a victory amidst adversity or temptation, a sealing with the Holy
Spirit. The word "seal" means that his presence seals us in
fellowship with God, seals us with a beautiful assurance of
salvation, and also seals us from the onslaughts of the demonic powers.

This understanding of being sealed with the Spirit is important for assurance in the life of the Christian. But it is not
that one is sealed *by* the Spirit as though this is some formal

act which leaves a stamp upon us so that we are free from encroachments by the evil one. It is rather that we are sealed *with* the Holy Spirit. It is "Christ in you, the hope of glory," as Paul says. His presence is the seal. He keeps us from the encroachment of the evil one. We, who are in Jesus Christ, know by faith this reality of belonging, of abiding, of the Holy Spirit sealing us in fellowship with him.

The word "seal" is in a very real sense a word picture. It is a symbol of ownership and of authority. In Paul's day when a person in a position of authority in the Roman Empire sent a message it would be sealed with wax with the stamp of Caesar. This seal was its security. Anyone tampering with the scroll answered to Rome. Just so Christ is our Lord through the authority which he received with his resurrection, and he seals his own with the claim of ownership. And this is not with a stamp but with the presence of the Spirit. He is our security, not a happening but a presence. Not an experience where you get something "finished" with God and then walk on. Our security is his very presence, laying claim to our total lives, glorifying Christ in us, fashioning our lifestyle after our Lord. He has an investment in us. Paul even calls it an "inheritance" and he is sealing us in fellowship (Ephesians 1:18).

We are sealed in or "into" a fellowship with God.

When we studied the baptism with the Spirit, we recognized that Jesus does the baptizing. The Holy Spirit is himself the baptism. In a similar way, it is the Holy Spirit who is the seal; "We are sealed with the Holy Spirit." That is, Jesus Christ, who gives us the Holy Spirit, seals us into fellowship with himself by the presence of the Holy Spirit.

First John 5:18 says, "We know that anyone born of God does not continue to sin; the one who was born of God keeps him safe, and the evil one does not touch him." This means that because of the presence of the Holy Spirit in our lives the devil can't touch our little finger without the permission of our Father God! First Corinthians 10:13 says, "No temptation has seized you except what is common to man. And God is faithful; he will not let you be tempted beyond what you can bear. But when you are tempted, he will also provide a way out so that you can stand up under it." God in Christ understands our limitations. Through the discernment and work of the Holy Spirit he limits the size of the temptation that besets us. He limits the temptation to the level of our spiritual maturity so that we know how to draw on his grace for victory.

When we are tempted and feel the weight of temptation, in one sense this is a compliment. God permits us to be tempted only to the level of a maturity which is able to appropriate God's grace to overcome temptation. There is no temptation, then, that needs to overwhelm us, for we can turn to Jesus who is the way to escape. By his Spirit we can find the power for victory over that temptation.

This sealing is a matter of God's keeping power. Jude writes, "Keep yourselves in God's love" (verse 21). If we keep ourselves in the will of God, he will keep us. It is the Spirit who keeps stirring in us the conviction and love which keeps us in God's will. James says, "The spirit that he caused to live in us tends toward envy, but he gives more grace" (James 4:5, 6). This is not to say that we may not deliberately, on our own, defy God's leading and put ourselves into situations that make sinning easy.

We are sealed from the onslaught of the demonic.
"Greater is he that is in you, than he that is in the world" (1 John 4:4, KJV) introduces another aspect of this sealing.

We are sealed in fellowship with God, but we also have security from the power of the demonic that would encroach upon our lives. In the disciple's prayer which our Lord taught us to pray, we ask, "Lead us not into temptation." Or, if I may paraphrase it, "Lead us not into situations that make sinning easy." The Holy Spirit, at work in one's life, sealing one in fellowship with God, seals us from the onslaught of the demonic. It is by his power that we can live in victory and say "no" to temptations.

There is an infatuation with the occult in our society today. Persons are obsessed with a fear of the demonic. Wherever there is a non-theistic philosophy of life the consequent emphasis on the demonic becomes apparent. But when our concept of Christ is high enough we need not fear the demonic. Paul says that Christ spoiled principalities and powers, he defeated Satan at Calvary and has unmasked the evil powers so that we will not trust them (Colossians 2:15)!

We need to be aware that Satan is not a second god in the world; he is not that great. He is much more powerful than we are, but he is far inferior to Jesus Christ. His demons may be strong, but in comparison to Christ and the Spirit they are but little pip-squeaks. "Greater is he that is in you . . .!"

This is the language of faith. To affirm that one is sealed with the Spirit and need not fear the demonic is a faith affirmation. This is hardly demonstrable any more than other experiences with the Spirit are provable, except as witnessed in a victorious life as evidence of his presence and power. But we claim this by faith, for in the faith which receives the Spirit in fullness in our lives we know his presence as sealing us in fellowship with God, free from the powers of the demonic. We should be so involved with living and walking in the Spirit that we do not give attention to the demonic. We honor that to which we give our attention; let it be Christ.

This sealing is spoken of as the earnest of our inheritance, the beginning experience of all that God intends for us to enjoy in his presence. When God is present in our lives by the Holy Spirit, we are enjoying now the meaning of membership in the kingdom of heaven. Fifty billion years from now, living on with God, will be an expanded dimension of what has already begun in the life of faith by the presence of the Holy Spirit. This enables one to be a realist about life, to be honest about the problems and at the same time be optimistic about the outcome. The believer stands with his hand in God's and with the awareness of the presence of the Holy Spirit in his life. He has an ability to smile in the face of adversity.

We often fail at this level of faith. Instead of being able to praise God in the midst of problems, we turn our mouths down at both corners and act as though honesty means telling the whole world about our burdens. Some time ago I was speaking to a high school audience where there was considerable emphasis on the matter of honesty interpreted as imposing one's gut-level feelings on other people, thereby discouraging them. I shared the comment that "a forced smile is still better than a sincere grouch." I do not believe it is fair, nor is it Christian love, to pour out all of one's feelings and hostilities upon another, thereby forcing the other person to carry that problem, and justify our doing so under the guise of honesty. We can be honest and at the same time be loving and respectful of others. We need to be discerning as to what we do in our relationship to others.

We have seen that the sealing with the Holy Spirit is, first of all, a sealing in fellowship with God. One walks in this assurance because the Spirit is present in his life. And second, it is a sealing from the onslaught of the demonic or Satan. We live with the assurance that the devil cannot overrun our lives. When your faith in Jesus Christ is high enough, you don't have to worry about demons. If you confess Jesus as Lord, then you simply affirm, "Greater is he that is in you than he that is in the world." We can trust Jesus Christ through the Holy Spirit to secure and safeguard our freedom.

To help persons oppressed by the demonic we can engage in intercessory prayer. This is not overcoming God's reluctance but overcoming the hindrances to God's work. God does not violate personality, but moves in proportion to our openness to him. Where demonic powers are oppressing persons, it is our privilege to invite God to move into their lives through us in a redemptive relationship. Intercession means that we defy the problem of sin or the power of the demonic as an effect on a person's life and bring God's power to bear upon them. One can deliberately put his hand in the face of the devil and say, "Stand back, my Lord is moving in here."

We are also sealed in his will for our character.

The experience with the Spirit is not more emotional than it is ethical. The sealing with the Spirit means that he would keep us from behaving in ways that are inconsistent with the love of Christ. As to love, the apostle Paul says, it "covers a multitude of sins." But this hardly means that one goes ahead and sins and charity covers this over, as though in love we don't notice those sins. We are all too realistic to think that. The verse may well mean "charity covers over our tendency to sin." When the Spirit of God sheds the love of God abroad in our hearts, that love covers over or blocks out the tendencies toward envy, jealousy, lust, ill will, prejudice, and hostility. We should pray for the love of God to abound freely in our lives. We should be asking the Holy Spirit, who fills our lives and seals them in the fellowship of God, to teach us to love. This new love of the Spirit is to become the dominant expression of our Christian character. Where the Spirit of the Lord is in freedom, this love will come through, for "God has poured out his love into our hearts by the Holy Spirit" (Romans 5:5).

This is not automatic, nor is it something static. The heart in Hebrew psychology meant the center of motivation. To enthrone Christ at the center of one's life is a conscious, deliberate confession. In that new relationship the basic element of this faith granted to us by the Holy Spirit is love. But love must be developed. And the Spirit works with us in ways consistent with the psychology of personality development. He does not violate the personality. Thus it follows that, if love must be developed, we must learn to love. It is like receiving a precious gift, but we must learn to use it.

We must learn to love beyond our insecurities. We must learn to love beyond our prejudices, beyond our own group. We must learn to love across racial and cultural barriers. Professor Nico Smith, speaking to this point at the South Africa Christian Leadership Assembly at Pretoria in July 1979, said, "We can't love one another collectively," we must learn to love individual persons. Jesus' compassion reached out to individuals.

Paul wrote, "For the kingdom of God is not a matter of eating and drinking, but of righteousness, peace and joy in the Holy Spirit" (Romans 14:17). The kingdom is more than little rules, the kingdom is the will of Christ, it is a matter of Spirit. And when we speak of righteousness, peace, and joy in the Holy Spirit, we are speaking about the spirit of our lives. When one knows the Holy Spirit and lives with harmony in himself, it is not difficult to live in love toward one's fellows.

Love as the motivating expression of our lives means an openness to relate with others in acceptance of their true worth. Love never manipulates another. Love doesn't misuse another. Love doesn't coerce another. Love is always respectful of the other. And love finds its full meaning when it helps persons to achieve complete fulfillment and meaning for their lives. Should we tend to use other persons, to rob them of the freedom to be themselves in the grace of God, we violate the meaning of love. Love fully expressed is justice (righteousness) toward others.

The Holy Spirit as the seal for our character is the power that keeps us from behaving in ways that are other than Christian. The Spirit has come to make contemporary the truth of Jesus, to make the work of Christ personal and powerful in our lives. By his love he enables us to live in love. By his holiness we experience holiness. In his joy we know inner joy, and "the joy of the Lord is our strength."

There is no gospel in advice alone. Advice is at the level of legalism. It is telling a person what he ought to do. One moves from legalism to gospel or grace by moving from the matter of compulsion to the matter of relationship. The gospel is not just advice, it is invitation. We do not offer good views but we offer good news. And the good news is that if you open your life to Jesus Christ he accepts you, he grants forgiveness, he moves into your life by his Holy Spirit and transforms it.

The Holy Spirit comes into our experience to call, convict, regenerate, and to guide us. When we open our lives to the lordship of Jesus Christ, to let him rule and be in control, then Jesus baptizes us with the Spirit. He gives us the Spirit to dwell in our lives, and his presence is the seal or assurance of our fellowship in grace. In this sealing the Spirit will do for you all that we have seen.

Jesus, the risen Lord, is at the right hand of God in heaven, but he purposes to abide in our hearts "because he has given us of his Spirit" (1 John 4:13). The kingdom of God is not just an idea, but is a new way of life for which the power has been provided. It is for us to open ourselves to him by faith and to one another in love. The kingdom is happening among us, and we can ask the Holy Spirit to do in us that which will make the rule of Christ real in our lives. Of this power Jesus said, "If you then, though you are evil, know how to give good gifts to your children, how much more will your Father in heaven give the Holy Spirit to those who ask him" (Luke 11:13)! We can ask him day after day for a fresh filling for each day. This is the good news of the gospel.

Many Christians seem to be immobile, inactive, as though waiting for the Spirit to come. He has come. He is here. It is good news that we can receive him into our lives. It is good news to know that Christ is present, that we don't walk alone. It is good news to know that his fellowship will continue to transform us. It is deeply satisfying to share the sense that God is doing something big, and that we get in on it. And he is—for Paul says that God is making known his wisdom to the principalities and powers in heavenly places by what he is doing through the church! (Ephesians 3:10). We are God's exhibit before the hosts of the universe of his redemptive work. Being sealed with the Spirit is our security in grace.

> Lord Jesus, each of us would open
> ourselves to the reality of your
> presence and appropriate this
> sealing by faith, to know your
> freedom, your love, and your joy.
>   Amen.

Study Questions

1. Is the security of his presence spoken of in this chapter as meaningful for us as is an emphasis on a security in divine election?

2. How can we become more realistic about being "inner directed" through the Spirit in contrast to being "outer directed" by constraint?

3. In what ways can we help persons find freedom from the demonic influences without exaggerating the demonic influence and using it as escape from our own responsibility for human selfishness?

4. What are some of the key expressions of Christian character imparted to us by the Spirit of Christ?

10
PRAYING IN THE SPIRIT

10
Praying in the Spirit

For in this hope we were saved. But hope that is seen is no hope at all. Who hopes for what he already has? But if we hope for what we do not yet have, we wait for it patiently.

In the same way, the Spirit helps us in our weakness. We do not know what we ought to pray, but the Spirit himself intercedes for us with groans that words cannot express. And he who searches our hearts knows the mind of the Spirit, because the Spirit intercedes for the saints in accordance with God's will.

And we know that in all things God works for the good of those who love him, who have been called according to his purpose. For those God foreknew he also predestined to be conformed to the likeness of his Son, that he might be the firstborn among many brothers.

Romans 8:24-29.

Prayer is worship, for it is reverent communication with God. But prayer is not overcoming God's reluctance, prayer is laying hold on God's willingness. Prayer is not talking God into doing something that he is hesitant about doing. Prayer is opening one's life to God, giving him the moral freedom to do in our lives what he has been wanting to do for a long time. God does hear and God does answer prayer, creating his people.

133

In November 1975, Esther and I had the privilege of being in Central America and visiting the church outreach in five or six different countries. There we saw a remarkable expression of how the Spirit of God is using people to win others to Christ and build a living and dynamic church. Here we saw evidence again of how the Holy Spirit works, creating his church.

In San Pedro Sula, Honduras, we visited the Amsey Yoders who came to the city five years before when there was no congregation there from my denomination. In a five-year period they were used of the Spirit to build a dynamic congregation which also had five mission outreaches. The congregation, alive and committed, had effectively crossed sociological lines, something which in any culture is very difficult. Their membership is made up of persons from the whole range of social, racial, and economic groups. It is a witness to the reality of the fellowship of the Spirit of Jesus Christ.

Our experience took us to the San Blas Islands, off Panama, where there is a remarkable testimony of what God is doing as he creates his church among the Cuna Indian people in very primitive surroundings. On island after island there is a fellowship of believers. The gospel has brought meaning, hope, and purpose into persons' lives. It has transformed those lives with meaning in a setting completely void of affluence!

One of the remarkable things about the spread of the gospel is that the Holy Spirit contextualizes the gospel for a given people. He is always there bearing testimony to the truth of the Word; and the Scripture, inspired by the Holy Spirit, becomes for any people a dynamic communication of God. As people hear they respond and pray. Wherever persons call upon God, even though they have very limited knowledge of the gospel, the Bible, and a limited ability to read, God hears their prayers and answers them. He meets people where they are and brings them into an experience of his transforming grace.

Similarly I have seen God answer prayer on the college campus in spiritual renewal. He has touched lives with a call to service which changed students' basic lifestyles. He has met us in problems as we work together as a faculty and student body. He has answered prayer in our financial needs as we pray for persons to open their hearts and give of their resources to help in the investment of education to prepare young people to serve Christ. I have seen him answer prayer in evangelistic missions, calling people to Christ, changing lives that could not be changed by any other power than the way in which the Spirit of God transforms them.

To talk about prayer is not mere theory, but witness or testimony. It is a fact that the Holy Spirit responds to the believer as he cries for help on the basis of the will of Jesus Christ.

This chapter opens with a very profound, difficult, and searching text. Paul affirms that the Holy Spirit shares with us, engaging us in prayer at a level that goes beyond our own understanding, "The Spirit himself intercedes for us with groans that words cannot express" (Romans 8:26).

Praying in the Spirit means recognizing the fact that God has already identified with us in resolving the problem.

In the Romans 8 passage, Paul says that our salvation contains with it the hope of the ultimate fulfillment of everything God has for us, which we haven't seen as yet. Because we have that hope, because we know that the ultimate fulfillment he has planned is already committed to us, we can draw on that fulfillment like drawing on a bank account.

135

"If we hope for what we do not yet have, we wait for it patiently. In the same way, the Spirit helps us in our weakness." That is, in our limitations God releases in our lives something of the future fullness.

God releases in our experience resources as we need them which are a part of his greater power. He can release such power at any given time, to any one of us, but none of us could carry the full intensity of what the Spirit of God can do. It would burn us up. But Paul says,

> In the same way, the Spirit helps us in our weakness. We do not know what we ought to pray, but the Spirit himself intercedes for us with groans that words cannot express. And he who searches our hearts knows the mind of the Spirit, because the Spirit intercedes for the saints in accordance with God's will.
>
> *Romans 8:26, 27.*

We need to be aware that this world belongs to God, even where it has been usurped by Satan. Paul says of creation that "for by him all things were created: things in heaven and on earth, visible and invisible, whether thrones or powers or rulers or authorities; all things were created by him and for him" (Colossians 1:16). And yet, when the devil tempted Jesus by offering him all the kingdoms of the world if he would but worship him, Jesus didn't refute his claim. But Christ brought his kingdom into the world to overcome Satan and his claim to God's world! We must never forget that he is an intruder, for "the earth is the Lord's and the fullness thereof." When we confess Jesus as Lord we are overthrowing the rule of the enemy. When we pray, "Thy kingdom come, thy will be done on earth as it is in heaven," we are overcoming the enemy. We cannot hand any part of this world over to Satan. Intercessory prayer is to take authority in the name of Christ and overthrow the rule

of the enemy. This is praying in the Spirit, with his discernment and power.

The thrust of Romans 8:24ff. is to expand our awareness
of the spiritual dimensions in which we share. While we are
limited in our understanding of the interactions in the "spirit
world," the Holy Spirit engages them on our behalf to keep
us in the will of God. Paul writes, "For our struggle is not
against flesh and blood, but against the rulers, against the
authorities, against the powers of this dark world and against
the spiritual forces of evil in the heavenly realms"
(Ephesians 6:12). We do not know all that this envisions, but
we do know that the Holy Spirit understands, and that he
engages us in prayer beyond our perception. Perhaps we
could simply say that the prayer of helplessness, of a complete surrender of trust in our own ability, and full dependence upon him is our greatest prayer.

The beauty of Romans 8:24-29 is enhanced by seeing the
larger context in which this text is found. Paul affirms that
God is for us (8:31), Christ is for us (8:34), and the Spirit is
for us (8:26)! There can be no greater affirmation, no greater
assurance. Prayer is not coming to God to coax him into
helping us. Rather, prayer is conversation with a God who
has chosen and called us, whose creative purpose is at work
within and around us, and whose ultimate purpose is to
share himself with us. Prayer is identification with him, it is
our affirmation of his will, our confession of his glory and
grace. As we worship, it is not that we bring something to
God but that we worship or honor him by receiving from
him.

The Holy Spirit always makes his intercession for us accord-
ing to the will of God.

For us to pray in the Spirit means that we must study the

Word of God and counsel together as spiritual brothers and sisters as to how we ought to pray about a given situation. Above all, we trust the Holy Spirit to give us wisdom and discernment so that we might pray in the will of God. This is a very delicate matter of discernment; a strong personality in a group may convince others that something is the will of the Spirit when it is not.

Jesus said, "I will do whatever you ask in my name" (John 14:13). Again, "The Father will give you whatever you ask in my name" (John 15:16). The key is to be certain what we ask is in the name of Christ and not in our own name. The Holy Spirit makes intercession for us in the will of God, not after our own will.

The discernment of his will is the disciple's more important search. Here we are dependent upon the Spirit's guidance in his Word. Paul says that "no one knows the thoughts of God except the Spirit of God" (1 Corinthians 2:11), making clear to us that the natural person does not grasp spiritual reality. Even our understanding of Christ is not after the flesh, that is, after a human way of regarding him (2 Corinthians 5:16), but is according to the Spirit. It is by the Spirit's illumination that we can understand Christ and recognize the cosmic significance of Christ as King of kings and Lord of lords. When we know him as Savior, Lord, and master in our lives, we actually begin sharing the "power of an endless life" (Hebrews 7:16, KJV). The new life in Christ, regeneration, is a recreating in us of that which is truly human, of that which reflects the true personhood which God intended for us.

The Spirit's counsel in understanding God's will cannot be disassociated from his Word. To separate the Spirit from the Word written would be to leave us only with the "groanings which cannot be uttered." He speaks through his Word, not from himself but from that which he receives from the Father and the Son (John 16:13). God is not capricious; although he continues his creative work in the universe (see John 5:17), he does not contradict himself. With a revelation in history which reached its fullest expression in Jesus Christ, the Spirit does not give a word other than the truth as it is in Jesus. Our prayer in the Spirit, prayer in the will of God, is prayer in the name of Jesus; it is prayer in and by his Word.

Praying in the Spirit means that we must discern the will of God and be humble enough to respect that will.

There are those who have the impression that to pray in the will of God means that you achieve a level of confidence and dogmatism that you order things from God! Such people often conclude that it would be a lack of faith to say, "Nevertheless, not my will, but thine be done." But the greater expression of faith and humility is that, after we have sought to discern God's will, we still say, "Lord, this is what I believe is your will and this is what I'm asking in the name of Christ; nevertheless, if I have mistaken it, not my will but thine be done." This is not a lack of faith, this is the greater step of faith. This is the ultimate affirmation of his sovereign right to determine the answer. Jesus prayed this way in the Garden of Gethsemane. He knew what the Father was asking of him. He knew that his hour had come. And yet, as he prayed, he laid his own will out before the Father and said, "Nevertheless, not my will but thine be done" (Mark 14:36).

Consider the story of the three Hebrew children who were confronted by Nebuchadnezzar and asked to bow down to his image. When they gave their answer, he offered them more time to think it over. They said, "We don't need to think it over, we know what God would have us to do and we won't bow to your image." When he told them that they would be cast into the furnace of fire, their response was, "Our God is able to deliver us out of the furnace of fire. But whether he will or not we don't know, but we still are going to be true to him." That is what we call biblical faith. We may not be certain what God may permit by way of illness, hardships, or suffering, but the one thing the Word calls us to is an affirmation that we will be true to him. No matter what he permits, we should pray, "Nevertheless, not my will but thine be done."

To pray in the Spirit means that we pray for his will, recognizing that the Holy Spirit makes intercession for us with groanings that cannot be uttered. He goes beyond what we can understand. Since the Holy Spirit goes beyond what I can understand, I must then admit my limitations and pray, "Nevertheless, not my will but thine be done." We trust the Holy Spirit to engage the divine power in conflict with any demonic powers that beset us, so that he can bring the victory and glory of God into whatever circumstances, trials, or difficulties that may be permitted.

Praying in the Spirit means we do not pray alone, nor pray according to our own wishes or ambitions.

To pray in the Spirit means to recognize that the Spirit is God present as his agent in the world. The Spirit as God's agent is countering the evil forces including "the prince of the power of the air, the spirit that now rules in the children of disobedience." The Holy Spirit engages the conflict between the kingdom of God and the kingdom of darkness. As we stand with the Spirit as children of God in the kingdom of light, we do not always know what he is doing to the powers of darkness; but praying in the Spirit means that we recognize that he is here to help us in our infirmities. Romans 8:26-28 carries us beyond our limitations in this spiritual struggle and introduces the will of God and the kingdom of God in realms where there is so much of the power of darkness.

Some who read Romans 8:26 imply that Paul is talking about the Holy Spirit speaking through us in tongues; that is, the Holy Spirit goes beyond our ability to verbalize and prays through us in ecstatic utterances. I see no reason for us to say that Paul is talking about ecstatic utterances. To the contrary, this is not very ecstatic. The groanings suggest that the Holy Spirit enters into the agonizing confrontation between the divine and demonic beyond that which we can share, beyond our limitations. He makes intercession for us, on our behalf, in our place, at a level beyond that which we fully comprehend, yet which we realize is confronting us. The remarkable promise of grace is that the God who understands the heart, who knows what is the mind of the Spirit, hears this and he answers.

The greatest answer to prayer is the sense of his presence. When the disciples had asked Jesus to teach them to pray and he had given them a model (Luke 11:1ff.), he concluded with an illustration as to how God graciously answers prayer. The ultimate answer is the sense of his presence: "If you then, though you are evil, know how to give good gifts to your children, how much more will your Father in heaven give the Holy Spirit to those who ask him?" In many settings the greatest thing the child of God can do is to bring the sense of God's presence into the lives and experience of other people.

In this sense we are always ambassadors for Christ, representing our sovereign in a foreign land! Our ministry of intercession for others is to ask of God for them what they are not in a position to ask for themselves. Just as the Spirit makes intercession for us, just so we should empathize and intercede for others. This is one aspect of the priesthood of believers. It may mean that at times we step into a difficult circumstance as a deliberate act of faith; in essence we are saying, Because I am here my God is moving in to make his grace known. The empathy may be "with groanings which cannot be uttered," but there is the ministry of his "presence."

The message is basically affirmation that, despite the limitations of our understanding, we are still not alone. It is like a child who doesn't understand all that he faces, but his dad or mother understand and move beyond his ability by finding resolutions which the child couldn't negotiate for himself. In a similar way as children of God we are so limited and yet the Holy Spirit moves beyond our limitations and our Father understands and answers.

> Heavenly Father, grant to each of us
> the humility to confess our limitations,
> to open ourselves to the Spirit and his
> dynamic power, to claim his work, and to rest
> in that work as he represents us beyond
> our limitation, sharing the marvelous
> freedom and victory of your grace.
> Through Christ our Lord. Amen.

Study Questions

1. How can "consciousness of presence" be distinguished from the projection of our own emotions or self-hypnotism?

2. Can we learn to pray more effectively by dialogue with the Bible?

3. What are the aspects of prayer which are most rewarding in the disciple's life?

4. How does one relate the will of God in the Word to choices of lifestyle?

11
THE ANOINTING OF
THE HOLY SPIRIT

11
The Anointing of the Holy Spirit

> But you have an anointing from the Holy One, and you all
> know the truth.
>
> *1 John 2:20, author's translation.*

Convicted and commissioned by God to carry out the
mission Jesus Christ is an awesome matter. To know that
God has called and anointed one to do his work is a sacred
trust. Such persons live with the awareness that Jesus and his
kingdom become visible to society through them. This conviction is confirmed by the Holy Spirit laying his claim upon
one's conscience. Paul speaks of this in his own experience:
". . . my conscience confirms it in the Holy Spirit" (Romans
9:1).

This study on the work of the Holy Spirit is designed to
help us understand how to enjoy what God has given us in
the presence of the Spirit. It is intended to motivate us to an
appropriating faith which moves beyond academic understanding or intellectual awareness, to reach out and relate to
the Holy Spirit. When we pray we do not only seek things
from him, but we ask for his presence and his anointing. The
anointing of the Holy Spirit is this chapter's theme.

145

An anointing is a designation, an appointment, or commission by God. It is so used in the Bible to designate special workers for God. In the Old Testament this was for the select few, for chosen leaders. But Joel prophesied of a day in which this would change. God said, "I will pour out my Spirit upon all people. Your sons and your daughters will prophesy, your young men will see visions, your old men will dream dreams" (Acts 2:17). Peter writes, "You are a chosen people, a royal priesthood, a holy nation, a people belonging to God, that you may declare the praises of him who called you out of darkness into his wonderful light" (1 Peter 2:9). Consequently the anointing commission is for all of us who believe. It is our authority in the service of Christ.

Terms are used differently by different people. This is definitely true when persons speak or write about the work of the Holy Spirit. By reference to the baptism with the Holy Spirit is meant the presence of the Holy Spirit in one's life. Jesus is the one who baptizes with the Spirit, and the Spirit is the baptism. The anointing of the Spirit, in contrast, refers to that special anointing of the Spirit for power in witness and Christian discipleship. R. A. Torrey, however, appears to speak of "the baptism" as an anointing for power. Certainly, there is no such anointing apart from the presence of the Holy Spirit, but in this study, as in the New Testament, the word "baptism" is reserved to express Christ's act of giving the Spirit to the believer. There are other words to be used for the Spirit's act of equipping. These words describe activity by the Holy Spirit within one's life as a consequence of being present.

By the anointing of the Spirit is meant that special endowment of power and compassion that he brings into our lives to achieve his purpose. As Christian workers we know the difference between witnessing under his anointing and simply talking about the gospel. We know the difference between a sermon that is preached under the anointing or unction of the Spirit and a sermon that is simply a lecture or a more formal doctrinal presentation. Ministers know the difference between preaching under his anointing and the times that they have "just preached."

The statement on anointing in 1 John 2:20 is problematic in the King James Version, but the original Greek contains a dynamic and remarkable promise. The King James translation reads, "And ye have an unction from the Holy One, and ye know all things." Some persons reading this have said, "If I have the anointing of the Holy Spirit, I don't need to study, I don't need an education."

Once John Wesley was confronted by a person who said, "God doesn't need your education." John Wesley answered, "And God doesn't need your ignorance." In every situation God may not need our education, but he needs us as persons who can become the best possible tools in his hands. We are responsible to grow intellectually as well as morally and spiritually. The issue is not whether one grows intellectually by formal education or as a person who, being alert, reads and dialogues. The question is whether one is honestly open to all that God would bring into his experience, expanding the borders of his mind so that his approach to life is informed. Such persons are not bookish or opinionated, but are compassionate, understanding, and empathetic. Liberated by the knowledge of the greater dimensions of God's world, one is at the same time humbly aware that the more we learn the more we see that we understand so little in relation to the larger dimensions that are to be learned. In such awareness one has humility rather than arrogance.

First John 2:20 should be translated, "But you have an unction from the Holy One and you all know spiritual things." This reading makes quite a difference in our understanding of the meaning of the text. John is speaking of the anointing of the Spirit to understand spiritual things, to have spiritual discernment. When one is born of God, when one has received the Holy Spirit into his life, he has an unction that enables him to understand spiritual things. Serving in evangelistic work, I have seen people come to Jesus Christ and become newborn Christians who immediately have a sense of discernment regarding the truth of God's Word. In their study of the Bible they began immediately to come with insights and awarenesses that often surpassed other people better informed. The answer is that the Holy Spirit had given them an anointing of discernment, an anointing of understanding. The Holy Spirit illuminates the mind to understand the truth. Note again: "You have an anointing, an unction from the Holy One and you all understand spiritual things."

Paul writes in 2 Corinthians 1:21 that this anointing which is given to us comes from God who has also sealed us by the Holy Spirit. Acts 10:38 says that God anointed Jesus of Nazareth with the Holy Spirit, evident in the unselfish way in which he released the power of the Spirit in his service. The anointing with the Spirit is the plus in any ministry no matter how able the performance. He anoints us for deeper understanding, for power to accomplish what God wants to do through our lives.

There are other specific references to the Spirit's anointing. First John 2:27: "The anointing you received from him remains in you, and you do not need anyone to teach you. But as his anointing teaches you about all things and as that anointing is real, not counterfeit—just as it has taught you, remain in him." This emphasis on the anointing of the Holy Spirit means that he guides us into the truth of the Word as we open ourselves by faith. Apart from the Spirit's insight and illumination we would only "know Christ after the flesh" (2 Corinthians 5:16, KJV). But when we open the Scripture to study it, we should pray over it and ask the Holy Spirit to illuminate the Scripture, to give us an anointing of discernment to understand it, to enable us with insight to move beyond the letter of Scripture to the spirit of Scripture.

When I came to experience a definite infilling with the Holy Spirit in my life, one of the first changes that I discovered was that suddenly the Bible became a living Book. It became a Word that spoke directly and clearly to me. Reading it with the discernment of the Spirit, truth almost seemed to leap out and take hold of my life. This is the meaning of God's grace, of encounter with God, of an experience with him in which he lays hold of us. This is not a legalistic religion in which one struggles to find and lay hold on him. Rather, it is God who comes to us. When one witnesses or preaches under the unction or anointing of the Spirit, one is experiencing what it means to be a channel through which the Holy Spirit reaches out to lay hold on others. God forbid that we should try to witness or preach as though we are simply trying to give a good message and then ask God to bless it. In witness we are only channels through which the Spirit of God reaches out to touch lives. We must honestly and humbly confess that it is only by his anointing that anything really happens.

Roland Hill, a great preacher of England, would often enter the pulpit and look up toward heaven and say, "Master, help, for if I speak not correctly what will become of me, and if they hear not correctly what will become of them?" And he would pray for the anointing of the Holy Spirit apart from which nothing of eternal value will happen. Everyone who has experienced this knows that we can only witness of this reality. I believe in the importance of Christian education through college and seminary, but it must be recognized that, beyond the knowledge which a person gains by the educational processes, there must be this anointing of the Holy Spirit. Without this we can not be very effective in the work of Jesus Christ in the world. It is incumbent upon us to pray for this anointing if we are to be ambassadors of reconciliation on behalf of Christ (2 Corinthians 5:20).

When Jesus began his ministry, his first word was a quote from Isaiah 61: "The Spirit of the Lord is on me, because he has anointed me to preach good news to the poor. He has sent me to proclaim freedom for the prisoners and recovery of sight for the blind, to release the oppressed, to proclaim the year of the Lord's favor" (Luke 4:18, 19). The emphasis in those verses is that he, the Spirit, has "*anointed me . . .*" Jesus carried this assurance through His life and ministry. In fact, this dominated his life all the way to the cross. John said of Jesus: "to him God gives the Spirit without limit" (John 3:34).

We need to do God's work in God's way by God's power. It is the anointing with the Spirit that makes the difference. If we seek to witness only by our own power we will soon discover that our words are only words. But when we minister under the anointing of the Spirit, we find that the Holy Spirit will enable us to use the right words with the right discernment and understanding. At times it may even be the same words, but quickened in the hearer by his anointing they produce his fruit. I have not always experienced this, but there have been frequent occasions when in witnessing I have had the joy of leading persons to Christ. Frequently a person has said, "It seemed as though you understood all about me and that you were talking about me in your comments." While I do not know the person, the Holy Spirit did, and of the many things that could have been said, he selected the right thing and the right illustration and brought it to mind.

We must beware of thinking that the anointing is only upon the minister of the Word. In evangelistic preaching it is especially satisfying to know that the same Holy Spirit who rests upon me as I speak is resting upon the audience doing his work in the hearer. When this truth became clear to me in my ministry it brought a new freedom. Too frequently conscientious persons have ministered under a compulsion that the power of the Spirit had to flow through them to the audience, only to find themselves tied in emotional knots, projecting their emotion rather than the urgency of the Spirit. We can discern the difference by consciously honoring the Spirit's presence and work in the audience.

I have experienced both approaches, having earlier been conditioned to believe that the unction rests upon the speaker as the primary channel to the hearer, and then discovering the freedom of knowing that the Spirit's unction is for clarity and compassion in the speaker but that he rests upon the hearer and is the channel of gracious conviction. This is a wonderful freedom for both speaker and hearer.

Jesus promised that, in the day when we stand before rulers or others who are asking for an accounting of our faith, the Holy Spirit will give us the words we should say (Luke 12:12). This is our assurance, that he works through us. We cannot walk into situations having everything outlined beforehand because of the variables that will be there. But we can come to a situation with the assurance that the Holy Spirit's anointing is with us, and then rely on his anointing in that occasion. I believe in situational communication or situational application of his changeless truth.

But another word must be said to clarify the meaning of anointing. This anointing is not just an emotional or mystical feeling of power. It is a sense of commission, of authority, of assurance. In the Old Testament, prophets anointed persons for particular service. The anointing was their commission, their authority, and when it became known by the people that they had been anointed there was a respect given them which gave them audience with the people. In Jesus' ministry this anointing was confirmed by those who observed that "he taught as one who had authority and not as their teachers of the law" (Matthew 7:29). Upon his resurrection Jesus said to his disciples, "All authority in heaven and on earth has been given to me. Therefore go and make disciples ..." (Matthew 28:18, 19). In these words Jesus delegates this authority to his followers. In doing so, he gives the Holy Spirit as the confirmation of this authority. The anointing of the Spirit in our lives is the commission, the assurance, the authority of presence which accompanies our witness. This anointing brings assurance to our speech as it did for the apostles: "When they saw the courage of Peter and John and realized that they were unschooled, ordinary men, they were astonished and they took note that these men had been with Jesus" (Acts 4:13).

The Apostle Paul tells us that we are to desire spiritual gifts (1 Corinthians 14:1); this anointing by the Spirit is an important one to be eagerly desired. Among those gifts are knowledge, wisdom, and discernment. As we pray for the gifts of the Spirit which are best for the situation in which we are serving, he will be our anointing. By this anointing of wisdom, discernment, or knowledge, our deed of love will be the relevant expression the Spirit uses to bring another into the will of Christ. This anointing will turn our wisdom into proclamation of the gospel. As Paul says, we should "be eager to prophesy" (1 Corinthians 14:39), for our greater desire should be to share the Word of Christ.

> Lord Jesus, we confess that apart from
> anointing with the Holy Spirit we are
> powerless. We ask that this anointing
> may rest upon us in your service, for
> the glory of Christ, and effectiveness
> in your work. Amen.

Study Questions

1. How can we cultivate an awareness of "presence" in our congregational assemblies?

2. What worship patterns may better reflect recognition of "presence," rather than give a sense of academic or doctrinal dialogue?

3. How does an open invitation for response relate to our understanding of the action of the Spirit among us?

12
WITNESSING IN THE SPIRIT OF CHRIST

12
Witnessing in the Spirit of Christ

In my former book, Theophilus, I wrote about all that Jesus began to do and to teach until the day he was taken up to heaven, after giving instructions through the Holy Spirit to the apostles he had chosen. After his suffering, he showed himself to these men and gave many convincing proofs that he was alive. He appeared to them over a period of forty days and spoke about the kingdom of God. On one occasion, while he was eating with them, he gave them this command: "Do not leave Jerusalem, but wait for the gift my Father promised, which you have heard me speak about. For John baptized with water, but in a few days you will be baptized with the Holy Spirit."

So when they met together, they asked him, "Lord, are you at this time going to restore the kingdom to Israel?"

He said to them: "It is not for you to know the times or dates the Father has set by his own authority. But you will receive power when the Holy Spirit comes on you; and you will be my witnesses in Jerusalem, and in all Judea and Samaria, and to the ends of the earth."

Acts 1:1-8.

Following the resurrection of Christ, he appeared repeatedly to his disciples over a forty-day period. During this time he "talked with them about the kingdom of God." This had been Jesus' message from the first, the announcement of the kingdom. He had told the crowd that "the Kingdom was among them" (Luke 17:21) because the Christ was there. Wherever the king is, there is the kingdom. The kingdom is where Jesus rules. In Acts 1:1-8 it is clear that the risen Christ is back in business!

The disciples asked Jesus if he would at this time restore the kingdom to Israel. Jesus' reply was to leave the matter of the little kingdom of Israel in the hands of God; rather, he commissioned them to be witnesses of him. This harks back to Jesus' words in the Sermon on the Mount: "But seek first his kingdom and his righteousness, and all these things will be given to you as well" (Matthew 6:33). Jesus introduced them to a new power and cause that would extend the kingdom worldwide; their concept of the kingdom of Israel would be placed in context of the larger kingdom of God. His followers were to receive the power of the Holy Spirit which was to come upon them and thus to become his witnesses.

The coming of the Holy Spirit contextualizes the meaning of Christ for us in our lives and cultural situation. The witness can be given in Jerusalem, in Judea, in Samaria, and in the whole world because the Spirit makes the truth of Jesus personal for us. He makes the meaning of the Christ a contemporary actuality in our experience. It is this rule of Christ in our lives which is the work of the Spirit. And this rule of Christ is the actualization of the kingdom of God.

The kingdom of God is central in the message of Christ. The apostle Paul told the Ephesian leaders that he had gone about among them "preaching the kingdom of God" (Acts 20:25, KJV). To announce that Jesus is Lord is to announce his rule. The kingdom of God is not just an idea but is a way of life for which power has been provided. The Spirit has come to confirm and extend this witness of Christ.

As the Spirit creates a new community of God's people in society it will be a people who model faith, love, and justice. God's people are commissioned to be God's servants in the world. We begin by converting individuals but we move to a community of covenant love. As Professor David Bosch said at South Africa Christian Leadership Assembly, "The church must begin with individuals or it doesn't begin, but the church that ends with individuals ends." The Holy Spirit not only deals with personal content but social conditioning, because people are social beings and he is saving people. The Spirit calls us to fidelity to Christ as Lord or we fail to be God's "commonwealth on earth," (Philippians 3:20, RSV) but he also calls us to solidarity with the world or we lose our relevance.

Jesus said, "You will be my witnesses." We are to introduce people to Jesus—Redeemer, King of kings, and Lord of lords. We are his ambassadors, representing his kingdom in an alien land. To use another figure, we are in the arena of the world; our act is one of love and justice, directed by the Holy Spirit. The world, as spectators, is being introduced to the meaning of the rule of Christ. We are not simply following teachings of our founder, but we are involved with Christ, presenting to the world the reality of his kingdom. His kingdom centers in his person; it is his rule in our lives.

How does the Spirit witness to the Lord Jesus through us? The fulfillment of the promise of Acts 1:8 is described in Acts 2. The Spirit is given to the disciples on the day of Pentecost, and Peter, standing up with the eleven, gave witness to Christ. The report says that in response "about three thousand were added to their number that day." The occasion calling for such a response was not only Peter's sermon, but the total impact of Christ's three years of ministry among these people, his death and resurrection, and the regal act of the risen Lord in giving the Holy Spirit. No wonder that three thousand persons responded.

Acts 7 also speaks to the witness of the Spirit in proclamation. Here Stephen, full of the Holy Spirit, addressed the people. His sermon appears to be far more developed than Peter's sermon of Acts 2. Stephen traces God's salvation history to show that God's covenant of grace introduces a new age, a new kingdom, a new peoplehood or community. This new people of God replaces or supersedes a faith centering in an ethnic tradition, an institutional religion, or a nationalistic identification. The Lord is creating his new people on the earth through the work of the Spirit. This is the promise of the Father (Acts 1:4). This is the mystery hid from the foundation of the world (Ephesians 1:3-10).

There are three primary ways in which we share the witness of the gospel: by the presence of the believing community, by the pattern of discipleship which expresses the character of the new life in society, and by the proclamation of the gospel interpreting the faith of Christ seen in our deeds. And the witness may be any one or all of these, and in any order.

Witness by the presence of the believing community models the new life in Christ in the social and cultural context.

If we see in the book of Acts a handbook for the interpretation of the work of the Spirit, we can discover some important things about the character of the witness of the early church. Jesus said that in receiving the power of the Holy Spirit the disciples would be his witnesses (1:8). In chapter 2, when the Holy Spirit came the community of disciples witnessed by their praise and by their proclamation. But as Luke records in Acts 2:41-47, the witness was that of the new community in obedience, in fellowship, in worship, in unity, in economic sharing. This witness was accompanied by a sensational pattern of social action. In chapter 3, the witness is in a deed of healing followed by proclamation. In chapter 4, the authorities confront the disciples; there is dialogue and proclamation, followed by the witness of the praying church putting into action a relevant social action program to meet the needs of the believing community (4:31-35).

The church is people, a people of God. The building is not the church, it is only the place where the church meets to worship and edify one another in the faith. The church is, as Paul writes, "a dwelling in which God lives by his Spirit" (Ephesians 2:22). The church is a community of the Spirit, in the world but not of the world, distinct from the world, but a source of restlessness in the world. The church is in conscious relationship with Christ, while being an expression and model of faith to the world. Speaking on "The kingdom of God and the kingdoms of this world," at the South Africa Christian Leadership Assembly, Professor David Bosch said: "Without fidelity to the kingdom of God the church loses her sense of being God's colony in the world; without true solidarity with the world she loses her relevance."

This new community is, as Paul writes, "to be all things to all people" (1 Corinthians 9:22). It is a fellowship where there is no "Greek or Jew, circumcised, or uncircumcized, barbarian, Scythian, slave or free" (Colossians 3:11), but all with their differences become one body under Christ. Following the Spirit's teaching in Acts it was not until Peter was with the Roman Cornelius that he saw that God's new community was open to all people (Acts 11). In chapter 13 we discover that the church at Antioch included Jew and Gentile, white and black. The solidarity of this new com-

161

munity is our identification with Christ as Lord, being baptized into his body by the Spirit (1 Corinthians 12:13). This unity is not based upon ethnic, racial, cultural, educational, or professional identifications. It is a common covenant with Christ.

As the church lives with Christ, maintains her integrity, and practices Christ's love, she is a salt to the earth and a light to the world. She can truly be the church in the world as a community of the Spirit, confronting society with the higher will of Christ.

Witness by the pattern of discipleship expresses in behavior the holiness, love, and justice which can bring faith to society.

While the word interprets the deed, it is the deeds of Christian action which verify the word. The word articulates the principles for a Christian lifestyle, but the deeds express the priorities which constitute such a lifestyle. Jesus said, "All men will know that you are my disciples if you love one to another" (John 13:35). Again, we are to "make every effort to live in peace with all men and to be holy; without holiness no one will see the Lord" (Hebrews 12:14). This is a new quality of life in relation to all those about us. It is a call to justice and righteousness in human relationships. This peace is not only our goal, but our foundation and our motive. This holiness is not only our aspiration, but our healing and our wholeness. This justice is not only working to correct perversions; it is also our willingness to suffer and restore the dignity and meaning with which God created every man.

Discipleship means living as members of the kingdom of heaven now. Paul writes, "For the kingdom of God is not a matter of eating and drinking, but of righteousness, peace and joy in the Holy Spirit" (Romans 14:17). The Spirit manifests the Jesus life in us who walk with him as a witness in society. This style of life means that things of the world have been relativized; that is, they have lost their absolute value.

In moral integrity there is respect for the ultimate value of every person, and the refusal to misuse any one for immoral reasons. In material things the disciple's emphasis is on sharing rather than on hoarding. As to position, or status, the disciple emphasizes equality and brotherhood, not a superiority or ambition. Jesus said, "If anyone would come after me, he must deny himself" (Matthew 16:24). Even our enemies are to be treated as brothers, for Christ died for them also and we want them to become believers. Paul says "worldly standards have ceased to count in our estimate of any man" (2 Corinthians 5:16, NEB). This is the witness of a new community of disciples whose commitment is to follow Jesus' commandment, "Love each other as I have loved you" (John 15:12). In the first century of the Christian church a pagan said of the Christians, "How they love one another!"

After the resurrection, and in direct relation to the promise of the Spirit, Jesus talked with his disciples about the kingdom. In Acts 20 Paul speaks of his ministry in Asia Minor as "preaching the kingdom of God." This is an announcement and a demonstration that Jesus is Lord. This is the witness of discipleship.

Witness by the proclamation of the gospel contextualizes the Word in a given culture to announce and interpret the grace of Christ as a basis for saving faith.

The history of the spread of the gospel is one of proclaiming the good news of Christ. Paul writes of this to the Thessalonians that "our gospel came to you not simply with words, but also with power, with the Holy Spirit and with deep conviction. You know how we lived among you for your sake, you became imitators of us and of the Lord; in spite of severe suffering, you welcomed the message with the joy given by the Holy Spirit" (1 Thessalonians 1:5,6). This passage combines proclamation and discipleship with the anointing power of the Spirit. This witness of the gospel was Paul's pattern, and in this way he planted churches across Asia Minor and penetrated Europe. The risen Lord said, "All authority in heaven and on earth has been given me. Therefore, go and make disciples . . ." His disciples live and witness under that authority confirmed by the Holy Spirit.

The power of proclamation to reach people for Christ is not dependent upon any particular method. Rather, it is a matter of communication, and this is an art which the Spirit helps us refine in creative ways, fitting our personalities and the context in which we share. The church has too many persons who copy methods and fail to be themselves in the relationships which they have.

Proclamation is pronoucing the good news, it is sharing Christ. And this is done most authentically among people we know and who know us. The integrity of our discipleship makes our words significant to our family, our friends, and then to others with whom our friends are the catalyst.

While Jesus broke down the barriers which separate people through the cross, people still create barriers. We as servants of Christ must get over or through them. Jesus said we would be witnesses first at "Jerusalem," with those closest to us socially, emotionally, geographically, and culturally, Next we are to reach into our "Judea," the regions which border our primary communities. And then we are to cross barriers to "Samaria," to people quite different from ourselves, and share the gospel. To move in love to people unlike ourselves involves a deliberate step. From here there is no stopping, for now the Spirit extends the witness into all the world.

The Lausanne Covenant presents a striking statement on the urgency of the task:

> More than 2700 million people, which is more than two-thirds of mankind, have yet to be evangelized. We are ashamed that so many have been neglected; it is a standing rebuke to us and to the whole church. There is now, however, an unprecedented receptivity to the Lord Jesus Christ. We are convinced that this is the time for the churches and para-church agencies to pray earnestly for the salvation of the unreached and to launch new efforts to achieve world evangelization.... The goal should be, by all available means and at the earliest possible time, that every person will have the opportunity to hear, understand, and receive the good news. We cannot hope to achieve this goal without sacrifice. All of us are shocked by the poverty of millions and disturbed by the injustices which cause it. Those of us who live in affluent circumstances accept our duty to contribute more generously to both relief and evangelism.

Study Questions

1. What are the marks of Christian discipleship?

2. How is your primary fellowship of believers a salt to the earth?

3. How can we confront the structures of society with the awareness of the will of Christ?

4. How can we hold evangelism and social responsibility together as Jesus did? What perspectives and understandings make this possible?

5. What is the strategy of confrontation that is most effective in evangelism in our context?

13

THE COMMUNION OF THE HOLY SPIRIT

13
The Communion of the Holy Spirit

May the grace of the Lord Jesus Christ, and the love of God, and the communion of the Holy Spirit be with you all. Amen.

2 Corinthians 13:14.

Someone has said that the church today is not being persecuted; it is being ignored. This may be true if viewed from a religious mind-set in a society where everyone is expected to "do his own thing." However, if one thinks of the church as people whose lives have been transformed by the Spirit of God, wherever those people live together expressing the joy and ethics of Jesus Christ, they cannot be ignored.

The theme of this chapter, "The Communion of the Holy Spirit," has to do with the fellowship which the Holy Spirit creates. We sometimes describe the church by such terms as covenant community, brotherhood, or the visible church. The term "visible church" means that when one's life has been transformed by the Spirit of God through his relationship to Jesus Christ, one is introduced to a visible fellowship of the newborn. This fellowship of believers is the visible expression of the kingdom of Christ in its present stage.

169

When we speak of the church triumphant, we mean the church as the body of people who have died and gone on to glory. We speak of the church militant as those of us who are committed to Christ and are serving aggressively in his program now. Some use the expression invisible church to refer to the fact that there are those of the church who have died and gone on to glory and are now the church triumphant. But most who use the term invisible church do not use it in that sense. They mean by the invisible church those within the church visible who are the elect, the truly saved ones. But this implies that the church visible is made up of a general populace, both saved and unsaved. I am using the term church visible to speak of those of us who are committed to Jesus Christ, bound together in a covenant of love as a fellowship of believers, who become the visible expression of the kingdom of God now.

The affirmation of the presence of the kingdom and the communion of the Holy Spirit need to be held together. The model of this communion is found in Jesus himself and his lifestyle. The Spirit of love will condition us to love, to relate in compassion and righteousness. It is as we do justice to those about us that they recognize the reality of the kingdom. Jesus said that the final judgment will be on the basis of our compassion to others: "Whatever you did for the least of these brothers of mine, you did for me" (Matthew 25:40). The communion of the Spirit, the great equalizer, calls us to a servant role in the spirit of the master. Jesus' life was one of service, "for even the Son of Man did not come to be served but to serve, and to give his life as a ransom for many" (Mark 10:45). Jesus' triumphal entry into Jerusalem was on a donkey, the mount of the poor and powerless, not on a victor's white horse!

The community of the Spirit stands in open contrast to

the spirit of our age with its status seeking, power struggle, and violence. The community of Christ is a fellowship of love, of equality, and of peace. The master was a nonviolent revolutionary who taught love for one's enemies rather than destruction, willingness to suffer and bear the cross rather than the use of force, and forgiveness rather than revenge. What Jesus promoted was a community of love and fellowship emerging from a radical change in humankind's thinking and ambition. And with this perspective the Spirit is at work creating a new community with the power to change society.

But with this affirmation we now ask, what creates this kind of covenant community? Dietrich Bonhoeffer, a great Lutheran theologian who died in a Nazi concentration camp, discusses community with profound insight in his book, *Life Together*. Community is a gift of God, it is a gift of grace, it is a work of the Spirit, says Bonhoeffer. Community is not simply a sociological structure. Community is a spiritual dynamic. Community is what happens when people are bound together by the Spirit of God, when people relate to each other not directly but through Jesus Christ. Community, or brotherhood, is a gift. One cannot coerce community; in fact, one cannot structure it. We cannot simply pronounce a group of Christians to be a brotherhood even though brotherhood may be a strong denominational emphasis. Brotherhood, or fellowship, is a gift of God's grace; it happens by the presence and dynamic of the Holy Spirit.

The church is a fellowship of redeemed sinners in whose midst the living Christ is present by his Spirit. We must remember that the center of the Christian faith is the worship of Jesus Christ, love for him. While the kingdom has ethical dimensions we recognize that God created a people for

171

himself before he gave them an ethic. This is to affirm the order of the first and second commandments, to love God first and then to love one's neighbor. The communion of the Holy Spirit will help us incorporate both aspects of God's will.

The apostle Paul prayed his benedictory prayer: "The grace of the Lord Jesus Christ, and the love of God, and the communion of the Holy Ghost, be with you all. Amen" (2 Corinthians 13:14, KJV). Significantly, the Apostles' Creed relates the phrases "I believe in the Holy Ghost . . ." and "the communion of saints. . . ." The concept of the communion of the Holy Ghost is an important statement in this reference and should not be minimized. If I can have communion with the Holy Spirit and he is a part of the Godhead, a personality, then I can talk with the Holy Spirit. I can fellowship with the Spirit. I can interrelate with him. I know we pray to the Father through the Son, in Jesus' name, and on the merits of what he has done, and he answers through the Spirit to us. But we also have communion with the Holy Spirit, the one who searches the heart and makes intercession. But the "communion" of the Holy Spirit is not an individualistic experience, for there is a corporate dimension in which the Spirit binds the believers together in communion.

Communion has to do with relationship of the essence of one's spirit. It is not a superficial relationship. At Pretoria, South Africa, addressing the South Africa Christian Leadership Assembly, Bishop Alphaeus Zulu of Zululand spoke to the limitations of conversing by saying that "the white man's conversation is primarily an interview, not a dialogue. He asks the questions, and doesn't equally contribute. An interview approach is still speaking down to the other person." Communion calls for a mutual sharing on a common ground. How then can we have communion with the Holy Spirit? It is because our common ground is the person and glory of Christ. The Spirit has come to glorify Christ, and as we do the same we enter the communion of the Holy Spirit.

This is one of the deeper levels of worship. In the reverence of praise we are expressing honor to God. Worship is not so much giving something to God as praise for what we receive from him in grace. Worship then becomes an attitude of life, a lifestyle. As Paul Reese expresses it, "standing up in praise to God." When our stance, our walk, our lifestyle is one of worship, this will affect the total order of our lives. Worship is not putting on a robe of praise when we go to the sanctuary and removing it when we leave. Worship is not choosing to believe when with the gathered church and forgetting the belief when in the secular orders of life. True worship, the communion of the Holy Spirit, permeates all of life with the sacred. We will note some of the implications of such a life of reverence.

The Spirit will psychologically correct our individualism.

He does this by creating a covenant of love, a ministry of compassion that respects our individuality without permitting us to be individualistic. We are psychological beings; he works through self-understanding, not apart from it. There is no approval of an individualism that is selfish or self-centered in the covenant community. When we know and share the fellowship of the Spirit we are no longer lonely, isolated individuals. We are part of a covenant community of love. This sense of brotherhood becomes in turn an expression of love to a lonely, frustrated person in society; such persons can be brought into the fellowship of the people of God. In this sense, the church itself becomes a part of the good news of the gospel, an extension of the love of the Spirit.

Paul said: "Now the Lord is the Spirit, and where the Spirit of the Lord is, there is freedom. And we, who with unveiled faces all reflect the Lord's glory, are being transformed into his likeness with increasing glory, which comes from the Lord, who is the Spirit" (2 Corinthians 3:17, 18). This liberty which Paul speaks of is a liberty of fellowship. The Spirit present among the believers works to create this freedom, this fellowship, this joy. Our communion with the Spirit is our relating to one another through Jesus Christ with the joy and freedom that the Holy Spirit releases among us.

This calls for honesty on our part because when we are selfish and individualistic we are sinning against the unity and wholeness of brotherhood. This calls for integrity, for where we are guilty of grieving or quenching the Spirit, permitting in our lives things that bring reproach upon his cause, then he cannot release the freedom that he would like to release among us. This calls for love in practice, for where condescension, rank, status, and prejudice are present, there can be no freedom of equity. The answer is confession, cleansing, and openness to God and one another.

There is an old story of a man at a prayer meeting who, when praying, said, "Fill me, Lord, fill me." Another man broke in and said, "You can't do it, Lord, he leaks." Too often we are guilty in the church of putting on a front, of wearing a mask. As has been said, "Two masks cannot have fellowship!" We must be willing to experience honesty, humility, and cleansing if we are to share the communion and freedom of the Holy Spirit.

Further, there must be a yieldedness that is ready to obey, to walk in his will, to live by his love. Peter referred to the

Holy Spirit "whom God has given to those who obey him" (Acts 5:32). Yieldedness to the Spirit's will is a prerequisite for social harmony. But this unity does not mean uniformity; it does not mean that we are carbon copies of each other. Unity comes from the Spirit who binds us together in spite of our differences. With all of our differences we become one body, one fellowship, one covenant community around Christ.

It is clear from 1 Corinthians 12 and 14 that the body of Jesus Christ is made up of many parts. All of these parts are different—one being the eye, one the ear, one the mouth, one the hand, one the foot. And Paul asks, "Does the hand say because I am not the foot I am not going to participate? Does the ear say because I am not the eye, I am not going to function?" The answer is no. The body functions in harmony with all of its many diverse parts, so that the whole makes one great impact.

One problem in the church is that we spend so much of our mental energy grappling with tensions and problems which divide us. Our energy ought to be released in joy, in freedom and in aggressive confrontation with the powers of darkness through our witness to Jesus Christ. How will we answer when we stand before God and he asks why we spent so much energy in petty gripes? This energy should be going into creative, constructive work in which we confront the world with the witness of Jesus Christ. We are to challenge the principalities and powers, the very structures of evil. We are to refuse to surrender this world to the master usurper, Satan!

The church is called to be a community of believers who live in the communion of the Holy Spirit, who walk in active faith, carrying out his work in the world. This is the realm in which we are called to live, to relate in love so that through us the Spirit can build the kingdom of Christ. We need to ask the hard questions as to how and where he wants to do his correcting.

The Holy Spirit will pragmatically correct our materialism.

We live in the material order and by handling material things, but we are to be free among this material world rather than to deify it by materialism. It is the Spirit who can correct this by calling us to live as managers of the material rather than slaves of it. He calls us to be genuine stewards, handling things for the true owner, regularly permitting the owner to tell us how to use them to build his kingdom.

He can release us personally from being slaves to things, from being dominated by gadgets and material securities. He will free us from the tendency to play God with the things we own. Above all he can release us from interpreting the value of life by material achievements. This will free us to love one another, to fellowship. It will free us for family and friends, for hospitality, and caring. It will free us for the arts, for a concert, for recreation. We can be released to be!

In mission we should not measure the work of God and the building of his kingdom by dollar figures. We should think more in terms of what it means to share the good news, to reach persons for Christ. Jesus himself taught us that one soul is worth more than the whole world. And now his Spirit would correct our materialism by calling us to live with the value of the Spirit realm, meaning the value of persons, of personality, and of humankind's reconciliation with God. We are called to be agents of reconciliation, not agents of preservation.

He corrects our materialism by a new morality, a new ethic—by a principle of love. When we say that the Spirit has come to glorify Christ in our lives, we don't mean this only pietistically, we mean this ethically. The Spirit makes our lives Christo-centric, not thing-centered. We know salvation in relationship with Jesus Christ, and similarly we know ethical norms and directions in relationship with Jesus. We relate ethics to Christology in the same way we relate salvation to Christology—we walk in the Spirit of Christ. Materialism is not answered by simply reducing the number of things with which we work, but by an inner change in our attitude toward things.

The Spirit frees us from materialism also by elevating personalism above the material. Jesus' teachings in the Sermon on the Mount always elevate the value of persons above the material (Luke 6:27, 28). Things are to be used for the glory of God in the well-being of our fellowman. In doing this the Spirit elevates wholeness above moralism. The communion of the Spirit is to develop whole persons, and this means a life of balance and integration. When one is obsessed by things he will be a dwarf in spirit. The Holy Spirit helps us establish our priorities, placing some good things that we have high on our agenda further down the list so that some better things emerge as having priority. He releases us socially by elevating love above "rights." The child of God lives like Jesus did—he does not demand his rights! Rather, he lives to help others at an expense to himself. The more one grows in love, in the spirit dimension of personality, the more one will be free from the domination of the material.

But freedom from materialism is not achieved by simply rejecting material things. It is not by being careless, nor shiftless, nor is it by choosing to live so simply as to not participate in the responsibilities of the material order. To be successful in business does not mean that one is a materialist. A business person may be expressing his gifts in diligent discipleship, as Paul writes, "that he may have something to share with those in need" (Ephesians 4:28). Of course, as a disciple, principles of justice will guide his business relationships, including equal employment opportunity, fair wages, and concern for employee families. But the Spirit can make him free in the role of the material just as the Spirit can free a professional person from idolizing status, or an academic person from idolizing rank or prestige.

With regard to materialism, the more common theme in the Bible is for the privileged to care for the poor. There are over 2000 references to the poor in the Scripture, calling us to help them in love, to seek justice for the cause of the downtrodden, and to help the suffering, especially widows and orphans. There is no single social concern as prominent in Scripture as the concern for the poor. As Dr. Ronald Sider says, "God is on the side of the poor." The sanctification of our material privileges will lead us to share God's compassion for the needy. His perfection is expressed in his not being a respecter of persons, but in his attention to the "unimportant as well as the important."

The Holy Spirit will intellectually correct our secularism.

The way one thinks is determined largely by one's presuppositions. The Spirit renews our minds by leading us to think openly about God. He enlightens our minds with a Christian world-view, that is a world-view focused by Christ. He thereby challenges us to see life holistically in its spiritual, as well as its human, dimensions. When Jesus Christ expressed the nature of God in human form, he demonstrated that God could become human without being sinful. Humanness and sinfulness are not synonymous. What Christianity does is to expand humanness so that we may understand that becoming more like Jesus Christ makes us truly human. He is the one truly human person the world has ever seen. The rest of us, as humans, are perversions, until we are corrected by the regenerating and sanctifying work of the Holy Spirit.

The difference between humanness and humanism is that humanism, like secularism, has become an end in itself. It makes an idol out of humanity and humanity's achievements. We act as though "man grown up and come of age" doesn't need God anymore. The modern world looks at atheism not as something over against belief but it looks at atheism as man's achievement to now live without God. It is man's self-sufficiency at the ultimate level of being his own god.

The Holy Spirit will correct our secularism by showing us that God shares himself with us not to limit us but so that we can become all he wants us to be in Christ. True, we can do many good things without consciously walking with God, but it is also true that no one can ever reach his best apart from God! What the Spirit of God purposes is to transform our lives into being the best possible persons we can be in God's grace. The Holy Spirit will correct the idolatry of our humanism by releasing the power of Christ in us. He will make us truly Christlike so that we express true humanness, caring, love, and the meaning of life in the fullness of Christ among our fellows.

Secularism also cuts the nerve of evangelism in the church, for it maximizes human achievements and minimizes reconciliation with God. Reconciliation is the heart of the gospel, the good news that we can be reconciled to God. At the same time, it is the heart of a full-orbed human experience in that we were created in God's image for fellowship with him; no one is a complete person without that fellowship. One of the greater sins of higher education is the confidence that by the pursuit of knowledge persons can become complete beings without God. Higher education tends to operate on the assumption that the secular realm is the broad realm and that Christianity is the narrower realm. It is actually the opposite; the secular realm is the more narrow, being limited to the secular, while Christianity can permeate the whole of the secular and in addition engage the whole realm of the spiritual. The Holy Spirit acts to correct secularism by refusing to let secularism claim wholeness for itself.

The Spirit's call for us to be agents of reconciliation includes the social dimension of the gospel. Evangelism which calls persons to the wholeness which God creates has an ethical dimension as an essential aspect of the proclamation. This means that service in evangelism carries with it an ethical motivation. First, where there is poverty of spirit or body, the higher ethic is for a ministry of correction. Second, where there is power to effect healing, there is a moral responsibility to minister to the need. And third, where there is perception of the cause, the supreme ethic is to answer the problem! The cause of humankind's limitations and social perversions is estrangement from God and consequently from one another. The Spirit wants to use us as a caring community, as a brotherhood of loving concern to be agents of reconciliation. This is the communion of the Holy Spirit, "writ large," extended to society.

Worship is a privilege, for it is acknowledging with gratitude the enrichment of our lives in grace. Reverence is the ability to retain the wonder of it all, of God's goodness in life, of love and friendship, of joy and togetherness, of peace and the pleasures of life. Worship is to place all that we are and have in proper relation to the one who keeps giving these privileges to us. And the communion of the Holy Spirit is to hold life's blessings in trust in a direct relationship to the giver and all of his other recipients!

Blessed Master, thank you for giving
us your Spirit so freely and graciously.
Forgive us for what we have done to increase the insecurity of others and to
advance ourselves. Take our heads in
your hands and turn our faces toward
yours that we may smile with you. Make
us Christlike in the whole of our lives.

Amen.

Study Questions

1. What are the sociopolitical dimensions of a two-kingdom theology, in which we take the kingdom of Christ seriously in society?

2. If the kingdom of Christ is expressed through the church being organized according to the will of God, what are the transcultural characteristics of the kingdom?

3. Can we identify priorities for the community of the Spirit as forms of the kingdom?

4. How does the way of love determine our behavior as citizens of his kingdom?

14
CONFESSING A PNEUMATIC MOVEMENT

14

Confessing a Pneumatic Movement

> ... those who are led by the Spirit of God are sons of God.
> For you did not receive a spirit that makes you a slave again to
> fear, but you received the Spirit of sonship. And by him we
> cry, "Abba, Father." The Spirit himself testifies with our spirit
> that we are God's children.
>
> *Romans 8:14-16.*

The Holy Spirit is in reality the sovereign God and he is
not to be manipulated. We do not initiate so-called "movements"—they are gifts of God's grace. To speak of the Great
Awakening, or of revival movements, or of the charismatic
movement, is better done in terms of recognizing and assess-
ing the movements of God rather than to feel that we can
stimulate such a movement. In speaking to Nicodemus Jesus
said of the new birth by the Spirit "that the wind blows
where it wills," implying by this that the Holy Spirit moves
as he wills as an invisible force achieving the purpose of God.
To honor and respect the sovereign movement of the Spirit,
we must be yielded to him rather than try to master him.

But a movement is something with which we identify, it is
the recognition of something which is happening which we
esteem as important, a cause to which we will give ourselves.

In speaking of a movement of the Holy Spirit, we need to be careful lest we seek to contain that movement or to structure it institutionally. He is sovereign, and we confess or identify with him.

One of the dangers of any renewal movement within the church is that we may soon become guilty of in-group identifications which are divisive. Patterns of "we-they" language develop, and thereby set a renewal group over against the very persons who are important for the continued enhancement of the renewal movement. This has at times happened in great renewals such as Keswick renewal, East Africa revival, and charismatic renewal. This is not easy to avoid, because in whatever movement one finds meaning, there his or her primary identification will be expressed. And with whatever symbols we find meaning, we will continue to champion those symbols as the conveyors of meaning. Even though God needs to use limited symbols at a given time to reach some of us, his intent is not that we champion the symbol but the reality.

There is an unfortunate tendency in the church today toward a polarity between persons whose positions might be described by two terms, the thematic position and the charismatic position. There is meaning in both of these positions, and there are limitations in both. We need the emphasis of the thematic position on a biblical theology which interprets the Holy Spirit and his work in relation to a holistic and consistent theology. On the other hand, we need the experiential emphasis of the charismatic position with its openness to freedom, praise, joy, and love.

We also need the dynamic expressions of the Spirit's work in the variety of forms characteristic of different denominations, lest we think of the renewal by the Spirit only in forms associated with Pentecostalism. This freedom to recognize the work of the Spirit in other and broader expressions has enabled the charismatic movement to pentetrate the larger Christian church. However, the movement has tended in the recent period to maximize particular forms and increase the distance between those who find meaning in Pentecostal forms and those who find meaning in other forms or symbols. It is possible that we have now come to a stage in which some patterns of the charismatic emphasis alienate rather than attract many Christians who are sincerely open to the work of the Holy Spirit, but whose preferences for symbols and expressions of worship are quite different.

Having had the privilege of attending the South Africa Christian Leadership Assembly, an unusually heterogeneous Christian gathering across racial, cultural, linguistic and de-nominational lines, I experienced an abundant evidence of the differences in a renewal of the Spirit. In this assembly the expressions of faith, theology, praise, emotions, and gifts were exceedingly varied, and yet there was a spiritual one-ness in Christ. In context there was no impression that persons with glossolalia were more spiritual nor that persons who raised their hands were better disciples. But each was free in his or her way to rejoice in the Lord.

In view of these and other factors, to conclude this study it seems appropriate to set forth a proposal that we recognize and honor a more broad "pneumatic movement" which in-cludes a God-permitted variety. In my experience of interchurch work I have discovered that there are times in which a more narrow movement has been a hindrance to re-vival rather than an asset. When persons are repelled rather than attracted by the forms of a movement they tend to re-ject the reality behind the movement. In setting forth a pro-posal for a pneumatic movement, it is my intention to affirm that we need an aggressive stance which honors the work of the Holy Spirit but which finds its focus somewhere between a more thematic position on one side and a charismatic position on the other.

It should be recognized from history that, while the modern Pentecostal movement is a rather recent phenomenon in church history, and the charismatic movement a very recent phenomenon, the various forms of the church's participation in the work of the Holy Spirit are as old as the church itself. We can study such movements from the first century to the present. The heritage in which I stand, the Anabaptist movement born in 1525 in the Reformation, had a very strong and clear emphasis on a personal experience with the Holy Spirit. The Anabaptists taught that a baptism with the Spirit was essential for effective and full Christian experience.

The movement had some of the typical excesses which have often accompanied revivals in different periods of history. A group of Anabaptist leaders met at Schleitheim February 24, 1527, to achieve a greater sense of unity in the Spirit among themselves and a greater clarity as to their stance and mission. As an example of their teaching, the words of Thomas von Imbroich are expressive: "There are two baptisms, the inner baptism with the Spirit and the outer baptism with water." This kind of teaching was not the exception but rather the rule in the Anabaptist movement. Comment could be readily made on the better known movement under the Wesleys, or on the Great Awakenings in America and beyond, or on the East Africa revival, but to name them may be sufficient for our purpose here.

It is important that we understand and recognize the dynamic of a pneumatic movement in which the presence of the Holy Spirit and his sovereignty is taken with all seriousness even though the forms in which the experience with the

Spirit is expressed may not follow the current forms of the more psycho-emotional manifestations. It is not the intention here to negate the validity of the psycho-emotional type experience, for many have a preference for this pattern of Christian experience and expression, but rather to emphasize that the New Testament does not support any one manifestation as the ultimate in the expressions of the work of the Holy Spirit.

There are five things which may well be considered as characteristics of a pneumatic movement. These are being set forth here as both a guide and encouragement to an appropriating faith.

A pneumatic movement will take the person of the Holy Spirit seriously, holding his presence in esteem above the gifts.

The biblical teaching is that the Holy Spirit gives gifts according to his own will. He gives these gifts to the church so that the total fellowship of believers may profit from the gifts. There are problems when persons associate a particular gift with a guarantee of the baptism with the Holy Spirit. In no way are these gifts spiritual status symbols for given individuals. In no way are these gifts to be interpreted in other than a biblical fashion: the gifts are given for service in the community of the believers and in the sharing of the gospel in the world. The gifts are not to be interpreted as mystical claims or guarantees of spiritual vitality, as is common among other mystical religions. The gifts are primarily functional for the enriching of the Christian community and the enhancing of its work. The important thing is the presence of God in the person of the Holy Spirit, and the recognition that he is here to glorify Christ.

A pneumatic movement will honor the lordship of Christ

above everything else, and thereby enable the Holy Spirit to do his work among us, for he has come to glorify Christ. Such a movement will take with utmost seriousness the person and presence of the Spirit doing his work among us to create a liberating community. His very work of liberating us as individuals will be confirmed by the liberty and freedom he brings into our fellowship to release one another in love. Jesus frees us, and although what behavioral scientists call determinism is still with us, it is not fate, only conditions, only determinations, no more! The community of believers which takes the Holy Spirit seriously will be a liberating community, a covenant of freedom. Such a community will also be released from a spirit of competition, jealousy, and of manipulation of one another. In contrast, there will be a spirit of edification, of encouragement, of love.

A pneumatic movement will take his community seriously, holding brotherhood above individualistic pietism.

The Holy Spirit creates community, a new fellowship where people who sincerely believe in Jesus Christ believe also in one another. On the day of Pentecost one of the greatest things that happened was the creation of a new fellowship. A new entity broke upon the human scene, and while this group went up to the temple to worship, it was a different group, for it was known as the ecclesia, the called-out ones, the church of Jesus Christ. The New Testament language speaks of this fellowship of believers as the body of Christ.

The church is a committed community with Jesus Christ as the head. The Holy Spirit maximizes his work by creating such a community living in a vital relationship with Jesus Christ as the head. A missionary friend of mine, who was especially enriched by the East Africa revival, said, "If you keep the head in its proper relationship to the body, you will not bite the little finger."

We must also recognize that the Holy Spirit works in and through fellow believers so that we become together an interpreting community. This community tests the sense of God's leading as expressed by various members of the group. The Spirit through the community overcomes our individualism while enabling us to express our individuality in the larger group. In a particular experience of sensing direction we can subject this "leading" to the larger group for testing through prayer and interpretation. This is not to be construed as purely a group dynamic, for it is the recognition of the Holy Spirit's presence in the group. Nor is it to be construed simply as a group vote, or achievement of consensus as a necessary attitude before the group can function. It is rather the open searching of the group in the presence of Christ for a confirmation of his leading. While this does not minimize the individual experience with the Holy Spirit, it broadens this to say that the authentic experience on the part of any one of us will be confirmed by the fellowship of believers. This latter is necessary if we are to avoid the individualistic idiosyncrasies about our particular experience which could in turn limit the harmony of the group in its functions.

The pneumatic movement will take sanctification seriously, emphasizing holiness above emotional freedom.

In any genuine renewal movement there is a sense of drawing near to God and a consequent sense of holiness. A movement of the Spirit will place importance on holiness of life rather than on legalistic struggles over rules. This is not to say, however, that holiness is without standards or disciplines. Rather, the disciplines of the Spirit are far more searching than the disciplines of legalistic regulations.

It is in the inner working of the Spirit that our motives are laid open before God, before our fellowship group, and before ourselves. It is in the experience of honesty that we can lay ourselves open at the level of motivation. Psychologically, all of us are a bundle of mixed motives, but we can consciously come to God and lay ourselves open to him with the integrity which says, "While I am not certain of all of my subconscious motives, consciously I will to do the will of Christ."

In the current charismatic movement there may well be too little emphasis on holiness of life. Whether intended or not, what often comes through is an emphasis on the celebration and the gifts of the Spirit rather than on sanctification and the orders of life in holiness. As a consequence, at times holiness has been misinterpreted or expressed as something which is more of an emotional experience or achievement than of a Christlike lifestyle. Holiness is fullness, completeness, the enriching and completing of the total personality in the image of Christ. It is not something which is achieved like a package and walked away with. It is rather a relationship of transforming grace which continues to change us more and more into the image of Christ.

A pneumatic movement will take ethics seriously, giving ethics priority over an experiential "happening."

The question is not simply whether one feels good about one's experience or not. The attitude of our times has been, "If it feels good, do it." Such a stance is a surrender to the subjective dimensions of experience, or in the biblical word, it is often the surrender to "the flesh." In Hebrews 4:12 we read that the Word of God is able to divide between that which is soulish and that which is spiritual. This divides between that which is motivated out of one's self-assertion or ambition and that which is motivated by the will of God.

Ethics has to do with norms—the discernment of what is moral or right. It is the expression of righteousness and justice, or justice-righteousness in life. It is the moral application of the wholeness or holiness which the Spirit of God is working into our inner being. Ethics is the social expression of the will of God which has become primary in the heart. As Jacques Ellul writes, there is an ethic of freedom in which we are liberated in Jesus Christ and stand in his freedom to become whole persons. This ethic of freedom enables us to relate to others in the will of Christ, to live by the norms of his kingdom, rather than to be determined by the mores of society or the status quo in our cultural setting.

There is a direct relationship between being Spirit-filled and being in the will of God. When this is understood ethics is an expression of transforming grace, not an appendage to grace. Christian concern for justice, righteousness, peace, and love is an expression of the Spirit's presence and sovereign work. He is building the kingdom of Christ, breaking into each culture and society with "a better way," challenging the status quo, calling us to something better.

In a day of global community we need his compassion. In a time of inequity we need his wisdom and strength for justice. In a day of violence we need his peace and love. In a culture of power and affluence we need a spirit of humility and service. The cause of human rights should have high priority among the people of God. In a time of nuclear armaments, we need a new conviction that will enable Christians to be nuclear pacifists, for a nuclear war could be nothing but madness. If we are truly a community of the Spirit, we will be a community of high ethical integrity.

A pneumatic movement will take evangelism seriously, placing witness above tradition and ethnic or sectarian concerns.

The God who loves the world loves all people. He is patiently at work to turn people to trust and obedience. By walking with God believers share "the power of an endless life." Evangelism is this sharing. Evangelism is making the message of God's love clear. It is making faith in Christ an option for all people. It is a caring relationship which demonstrates the spirit of Christ.

Evangelism is not program so much as presence, it is not logic so much as love, it is not persuasion so much as compassion. Our model is Jesus himself, who loved persons, identified with them in whatever their station or rank, and thereby introduced to them the Father. Jesus said, "As the Father has sent me, so send I you." The greater work of the Spirit is reconciling persons to God through the covenant of Christ. This inaugurates the new life, the realities of the new birth.

We need to discover how the priesthood of believers can be applied in all of life, how we can be a priest at our neighbor's elbow, how we can help anyone anywhere to faith in Christ and to baptism. Evangelism is not building our program but is helping persons to new life in Christ.

This study has been an attempt to highlight a position which will not be shaped by the extremes on either side but will be positive and dynamic. A thematic position is primarily conceptual, and is not relational enough to achieve the spiritual dynamic needed. A charismatic position is relational and emotional, but is not conceptual and ethical in adequate ways to provide the quality of worship and witness that best represents the New Testament. However, in expressing a pneumatic position which would stand between these, absorbing the best of each and yet focusing on the primacy of the person of the Spirit, we must recognize that he determines the character of his movement. We must remember that the Holy Spirit is sovereign and we should not seek to manipulate him. It is important for us to understand his leading, to recognize how he works through his Word, and to submit ourselves to his sovereign will.

The Spirit comes to glorify Christ. Any genuine movement of the Holy Spirit will be Christ-centered in praise and practice.

> May the grace of our Lord Jesus Christ,
> the love of God the Father,
> and the fellowship of his Spirit,
> be with you now and forevermore.
> Amen.

Study Questions

1. How do the symbols used in various movements condition us to select that which we will experience?

2. What are some of the creative forms of community which can have relevance in a changing society?

3. What are some of the ethical concerns which the Spirit is speaking to in our immediate community?

4. Can we exercise the priesthood of believers amidst the isolationism in our social context?

Myron S. Augsburger is a pastor, evangelist, theologian, and former college president.

During the past twenty years, he has conducted evangelistic crusades and preaching missions in major cities in the United States and Canada, as well as in Jamaica, Europe, the Middle East, India, Africa, the Orient, Central and South America. Most of the evangelistic crusades are scheduled under the auspices of Inter-Church, Inc., and sponsored by local interdenominational groups.

In 1980 he concluded 15 years as president at Eastern Mennonite Seminary, College, and High School (Harrisonburg, Virginia).

Augsburger holds degrees from Union Theological Seminary (Richmond, Virginia), Eastern Mennonite Seminary, Goshen Biblical Seminary, and Eastern Mennonite College. He has done postgraduate work at George Washington University, University of

Michigan, University of Basel (Switzerland), and Oxford University. He was a Visiting Fellow at Princeton Seminary, 1980-81.

His previous books include *Faithful unto Death* (Word Books), *Walking in the Resurrection* (Herald Press), and *Quench Not the Spirit* (Herald Press).

Myron and his wife, Esther, are engaged in a church planting mission in Washington, D.C.—the Washington Community Fellowship—as a visible expression of the presence of the Spirit in the nation's capital. They are the parents of John; Michael; and Marcia (Augsburger) Bishop.